WHOLARIAN VISION

Also by Katrina Mayer, PhD

The Mustard Seed Way

WHOLARIAN VISION

HOW TO REMEMBER YOUR CONNECTION TO EVERYTHING

KATRINA MAYER, PHD

IUNIVERSE, INC.
BLOOMINGTON

Wholarian Vision
How to Remember Your Connection to Everything

iUniverse books may be ordered through booksellers or by contacting:

iUniverse
1663 Liberty Drive
Bloomington, IN 47403
www.iuniverse.com
1-800-Authors (1-800-288-4677)

ISBN: 978-1-4502-9413-3 (sc)
ISBN: 978-1-4502-9415-7 (dj)
ISBN: 978-1-4502-9414-0 (ebk)

Printed in the United States of America

iUniverse rev. date: 4/22/2011

To Dhyana

and to Morgan and Maggie…

who remind me daily of the
mystical, magical magnificence
of being.

CONTENTS

FOREWORD

Have you ever had this experience? You are introduced to someone, and you immediately sense a strong connection. You feel like long-lost friends. As you talk and get to know each other, you find you have much in common and communicate with great ease. There is a bond and a comfort level that defies the short time you have been acquainted, and you experience a deep-down feeling that you have actually known each other a long time.

Now imagine having that feeling more often. Imagine recognizing each person you encounter as a long-lost friend and being comfortable talking to people you never met before. Imagine a world where no one is truly a stranger, and we all recognize our connections to one another. I am personally excited by that possibility and look forward to experiencing a world full of friends.

The good news is… it is possible. What I just described is the concept behind *Wholarian Vision*. Even though you may not have heard of it before, the idea has been around forever. Ancient philosophers spoke of our connection to each other and our oneness. Most religions refer to the beginnings of all life starting from a single entity. Even science backs the belief that everything in the universe originated from a single point in time and space. But contrary to philosophy, religion, and science, we have lived as if our independence is more important than our interdependence. We have seen ourselves as completely separate from one another. And, more often than not, we have focused on our differences rather than our similarities.

Lately, we have all witnessed the advent of environmental shifts, the continuation of global conflicts, and the results of unprecedented man-made disasters, all shrouded by a general dis-ease permeating our societies. Much of this stems from the human persistence to make decisions from a viewpoint of separation, not oneness. Rather than making choices that benefit the whole, choices are made to benefit a specific group. Instead of thinking of the long-term ramifications to the planet and future inhabitant, thoughts are focused on immediate goals and ego-driven agendas.

But we have a choice. We can change this thought process now. By incorporating Wholarian Vision into our daily lives, we can reverse these trends and begin to see ourselves as part of a greater entity. As Wholarian visionaries, we bring a global perspective to our decision making process, which helps us all make healthier and more meaningful choices. And, by recognizing ourselves as part of the whole, we are less likely to try to cross the finish line alone and more likely to do what is best for the entire team.

As a seminar leader, filmmaker, and writer, I love to inspire people in every area of their lives. And leaving this world a better place for my two beautiful daughters is one of my greatest hopes and dreams. I truly believe that if we all realized our interconnectedness and lived our lives with Wholarian vision, we would accomplish this goal. I have no doubt that oneness is the true reality, and we need to wake up to the concept in order to create a more sustainable way of life for ourselves and for future generations.

One of my favorite mantras is, "All that I see is me." Quite simply, this is what *Wholarian Vision* is all about. As each one of us awakens to this reality, we realize the power of One... One love... One life... One world.

Isaac "Ike" Allen
Founder, AVAIYA

ACKNOWLEDGMENTS

The first person I want to thank is *you*! That's right... I thank *you* because without you, the vision is incomplete. We are all part of the whole, so I send each and every one of you my deepest gratitude.

And where would any of us be without our families? To my mom, dad, and brother, I have enormous appreciation for the editing, critiquing, supporting, and nurturing you have done over the years, each in his or her unique way. I wouldn't be here without you guys!

To Peter, I give my eternal love and thanks for helping make so many dreams come true.

To Ike Allen, I send much gratitude for believing in this project during the early stages. That encouragement was invaluable!

To Lou, thanks for making the photographic experience a pleasure.

To my old friends and new friends, I thank you for guiding me on my journey and encouraging me in my process. I can't thank you enough for your wisdom and presence.

To the Vangels... you women *rock*!

And to all the inspiring, encouraging, loving, and caring spirits I have met through Facebook, you truly make the world a better place.

Many blessings to you all!

INTRODUCTION

As a child, I loved reading the Danny Dunn series of books. Danny is a bright, rambunctious boy who handles every predicament with a scientifically based answer or escape. Of course, it helps that Danny lives in a house owned by a bumbling professor who gives him plenty of reasons to get in trouble. And you can be sure that Danny and his two friends find themselves in trouble often.

The last book in the Danny Dunn series was *Danny Dunn and the Universal Glue*. Professor Bullfinch created a glue that would have made Elmer's and 3M mighty jealous. This glue was more powerful than any other glue ever invented and could stick anything together. Professor Bullfinch said of this adhesive, "It will hold two separate pieces of something as firmly as if they were one piece. It will even—if you can imagine such a thing—stick two pieces of water together... "In fact," the professor finished, "you might call it universal glue."

Danny and his friends go on to save the day by using the glue to mend a cracked dam. They also expose a local factory that is leaking unfiltered waste water into the aquifer and make them admit their wrongdoing. But more than these heroic efforts struck me in Danny's story. It is the idea of this super glue that really got my attention. What a great analogy the glue is to the connection we all have to one another. We are all "stuck" together with universal glue! And Professor Bullfinch didn't invent it in his laboratory. Universal glue isn't fiction. It's real!

Maybe it was that long-ago memory of the Danny Dunn book, or maybe not. But I had an unusual word stuck in my head like glue when I woke up one morning at 4:00 a.m. Over and over the word repeated, until I promised myself I would research its meaning when I got up the next morning. By 7:30 a.m., I was on the computer doing a search, only to find out that... the word in my head didn't exist.

What? How could that be? I knew what the word meant with absolute certainty. I also knew the relevance of the word in my life and in the world. And yet, every online search came up empty.

Thus, the word *Wholarian* was born in the summer of 2008. And with it came the understanding that I would share it, and its meaning, with all of you. The writing of this book is a big part of that vision. And each time I sat down to write, the words and ideas flowed through me like water flowing through a tap. But I tried to capture all the precious drops and get them on paper in order to share with you.

So, I present the Wholarian concept. Just think of it as being connected to all things and all people with Professor Bullfinch's universal glue. Sounds far-fetched and preposterous? Then keep reading, and you will see that this concept is quite believable and older than time itself. And once you begin to truly see the world with Wholarian Vision, it will become apparent that the evidence has been in front of your eyes all along.

SECTION ONE

THE CONCEPT

It no longer serves us to believe that we are separate from each other.
We are undeniably connected to all things,
and all people, both seen and unseen.
And as we acknowledge these connections... we are healed.

CHAPTER ONE

IN THE BEGINNING

ONE

We'll start
from the beginning…
and in the beginning there was… One.
Nothing existed other than One
completely, perfectly
One

Then,

in a flash of

inspiration,

generation,

creation,

divination,

imagination,

vibration,

transformation,

celebration,

and pair formation,

One became…

many.

And the many quickly forgot they were part of
One.

"One" has been known by different names as well as forms. From Omnipotent God to Cosmic Egg, from Tree of Life to Earth Mother, from Creator to Big Bang, the list is long as well as imaginative. Just as long is the list of creation stories illustrating how One became many. But, regardless of religion, tradition, culture, or scientific perspective, each story begins with One, and from One all things are formed. That is how it all began.

Let's look at some of the major creation stories. Many of these are familiar and show us how One became many. In Christianity and Judaism, the story begins in the Old Testament: "In the beginning God created the heavens and the earth" (Genesis 1:1).

According to the Bible, heaven and Earth did not exist before God created them. Neither did light, sky, land, seas, vegetation, sun, moon, stars, fish, birds, animals, or man. God created all these things in six days and rested on the seventh. The One God created everything.

In Chinese tradition, it is written in the Tao Te Ching, "The Way gave birth to unity, Unity gave birth to duality, Duality gave birth to trinity, Trinity gave birth to the myriad creatures. The myriad creatures bear yin on their backs and embrace yang in their bosoms. They neutralize these vapors and thereby achieve harmony." The myriad creature came from the Way... the One.

Hindus believe the universe was created from the Word "Om" and that nature and all of God's creations are manifestations of him. Hence, all animals and humans have a divine element in them. Om is the One.

In Sikhism, all that existed before creation took place was God and God's Will. God is the One.

And in Islamic tradition, according to the Qur'an, the skies and the earth were joined together as one "unit of creation," after which they were "cloved asunder." Again, everything was One until it split apart into the many.

Regardless of all the other differences in our world's major religions, they all generally agree on the fact that everything was made or created from a place of unity.

All that was created came from One. Let's repeat that. *All* of the something that we can see and can't see was created from the One.

Then, when we apply logic to this theory, everything that came after the original something is still connected to the original something because, after all, they all came from the same place. The One.

Make sense?

No matter how you slice it, we all come from the same place. We all come from the same One. Logically, that means we are all made up of the same "stuff." Hence, we are all connected.

Of course, there are people who do not think of the origins of our universe from a religious point of view. For those people, religious stories are allegorical but not factual. If that describes you, then you have the Big Bang theory. That is the creation theory that is supported from a scientific perspective. And lo and behold, you will find that it has the same basis as the religious stories.

According to the Big Bang theory, an intensely hot, high-pressure, astronomically dense set of circumstances existed, which resulted in a tremendous explosion. Then, over a great amount of time and space, heating and cooling, and expanding and contracting, the universe was born. Interestingly enough, no amount of science has determined what might have existed before the Big Bang produced matter. Where did the "stuff" that formed the universe come from, and what led to the explosion? But regardless of the answer, everything we now see or don't see in our universe comes from that initial matter. *Everything*! There is nothing you can see, feel, touch, taste, breathe, hear, etc. that didn't come from that initial matter. Sound familiar?

So what does this all mean? It means we are all part of the whole! We are part of the One!

Each of us is made up of the same stuff. We are all about 70 percent water and the proportions of the rest of the elements in our bodies are also similar from human to human. It is worthy to note that the surface of the earth is covered by 70.8 percent water. And the components in our soil are very similar to the components in our bodies. This is not coincidence.

Yet we continually see each other and the world around us as separate and vastly dissimilar. We easily rattle off twenty differences between ourselves and the person sitting next to us on the bus. One political party swears that they share no similarities with the other political party and vice versa. And we know for a fact that the person who thoughtlessly cut in front of us on the checkout line couldn't possibly have anything in common with us or anyone else on this planet.

But the evidence is there. Whether you believe in religious or scientific origins, we all come from the same place. We all have the same materials in our bodies that are in the trees, the rocks, the oceans, and even in the stars.

Carl Sagan, the American astronomer, astrophysicist, and author said it best: "We are star stuff that has taken its destiny into its own hands."

*_*_*_*_*_*_*_*

Let's remember a time
When I knew you as my friend
Let's remember a time
When our connection didn't end

Let's remember the time
When our lives were intertwined
Let's remember the time
When we had One loving mind

Let's remember that time
When you and I were One
When we were earth and sky and stars
When we were the light of the sun

*_*_*_*_*_*_*_*

The Bird's Nest

Hannah was young when her mother passed away, and she didn't have many memories of her. But she remembered that her mother smelled like spring flowers in the morning when she came to wake her up. She also remembered that her mother made delicious pancakes on Sundays. And she especially remembered how tenderly her mother would comb her hair every evening before bedtime. Her mother whistled a funny little tune as she combed, and never tugged or pulled as she worked out the knots one by one. Because Hannah liked to play outside, she often came home with small sticks or pieces of leaves in her hair after rolling on the ground. But her mother never scolded or complained and spent as much time as she needed to get Hannah's long hair smooth and golden blonde again. This was Hannah's favorite memory.

After her mother was gone, Hannah's aunt stayed in the house for a while. She helped Hannah with her hair. But after her aunt left, there was no one to comb her hair anymore. Her father was sad a lot and promised to help, but he often forgot. Hannah wasn't mad, because she knew that he missed her mother as much as she did. And her brother just yelled at her and said that he didn't want to help her with something so "girly." He didn't seem sad, but Hannah thought she heard him crying at night when no one was listening. So she wasn't mad at him either.

One day, she decided to ask an older girl who lived down the block to help her. Hannah always admired the older girl's pretty hair, so she thought that combing would be easy. Unfortunately, the older girl didn't have much patience to work gently through Hannah's knots. She pulled and tugged until Hannah's eyes were filled with tears. Then the older girl stopped and said she couldn't do anymore because there were too many pieces of twigs and leaves in Hannah's hair. She walked away, leaving Hannah with the comb stuck in a knot in her hair. Hannah missed her mother more than ever.

Hannah realized that she couldn't wait for her father or brother to help with her hair. And the older girl tried, but that didn't work. So she only had one alternative. She would have to do it herself.

She took her comb and went into her backyard to sit by the tree her mother had planted. She put the comb in her hair and immediately felt a big knot. She tugged and tugged and strands of hair came out, but the knot didn't go away. After about ten minutes she stopped because her head hurt and she only got one little knot out. So, she decided that each day she would sit by the tree and work on her hair until all the knots were out.

And that's what she did. Each day, Hannah took her comb and sat by the tree and worked on the knots. As time went on, she learned to be gentle with her hair and not tug so hard. A few strands fell out each time, but soon she was able to get the comb through her whole head and there were no knots left. That day happened to be a Sunday, and she missed the taste of her mother's pancakes. She cried softly as she combed her long, golden hair and hoped her mother was looking down at her from heaven.

She said out loud, "Look, Mom, I'm a big girl now. I can comb my hair all by myself. But I miss you so much."

And then she heard a funny little whistle from high up. It sounded like the song that her mother whistled as she used to comb Hannah's hair. She looked in the tree and saw a bird and realized that the bird was whistling that tune. And next to the bird was an amazing sight. It was a nest that had been woven with the golden strands of Hannah's hair. The bird must have picked up the hairs each day after Hannah was done combing and placed them in the nest. The way the sun shined on it made it glitter like gold. Hannah couldn't believe her eyes or ears because the bird kept whistling that funny little tune, just like her mother.

That is when Hannah knew that her mother was always with her. She was in the tree, in the bird, and in the nest that glistened so beautifully. She realized that her mother would always be part of her life and would be there to help her. All Hannah had to do was look around to see where she was. She felt like this was a new beginning. Nothing could ever separate her from her mother again, and that thought made Hannah very happy.

With a big smile on her face she went back into the house to ask her dad if they could make pancakes.

CHAPTER TWO

THE SEPARATION MYTH

A human being is part of the whole, called by us "universe," a part limited in time and space. He experiences himself, his thoughts and feelings, as something separate from the rest—a kind of optical delusion of consciousness. This delusion is a kind of prison for us, restricting us to our personal desires and to affection for a few persons nearest to us. Our task must be to free ourselves from this prison by widening our circle of compassion to embrace all living creatures and the whole of nature in its beauty.
—Albert Einstein

Within all of us is a varying degree of space lint and star dust, the residue from our creation. Most of us are too busy to notice it, and it is stronger in some than others. It is stronger in those of us who fly and is responsible for an unconscious, subtle desire to slip into some wings and try for the elusive boundaries of our origins.
—K.O. Eckland, "Footprints on Clouds"

The universe is simmering down, like a giant stew left to cook for four billion years. Sooner or later we won't be able to tell the carrots from the onions.
—Arthur Bloch

TWO

We all began our journey in this lifetime attached by umbilical cords to our mothers. Everything we needed for our bodies to live and grow flowed through those cords. For nine months, they supplied us with oxygenated, nutrient-rich blood. Then, during the birthing process, our cords were cut, and we were separated from the only world we knew. We went from womb to world, and the shift was immense. We were removed from a simple, enveloping, dark, comforting place to a bright, dry, chaotic world. No wonder we screamed.

So, our life experience was punctuated at an early stage with a profound feeling of separation.

And this sense of separation played out time and time again throughout our lives. When we were placed alone in a crib at night to go to sleep, we felt separated. When we were left in an unknown classroom for our first day of school, we felt separated. When a parent left the house to go to work, we felt separated. When our family moved to a new neighborhood, we felt separated. When a relationship ended, we felt separated. When a loved one died, we felt separated.

Wouldn't it have made all of these experiences less painful if we were taught early on that we were never truly separated? We were, and are, connected to all that exists. We are part of the oneness that existed since the beginning of time.

What exactly is the reason for perpetuating this sense of separation? Why would it benefit us to feel that we are not connected to one another?

There is a moment that I call the Big Bang of the spiritual world. It is similar to the Big Bang theory of our universe mentioned in the first chapter and may even be considered one and the same. Before this event, we all existed together as one, harmoniously. No separation existed, and everything was at peace.

Then, perhaps it was an atom, or a speck, a molecule, or a minute piece of the whole that speculated for a split second what it would be like to not be part of that Oneness. It vibrated a little differently and wondered how it would feel to be unique, different, or separate. It may have questioned its place in the totality. And upon this thought or this question...

~-BANG-*~*

The illusion of separation was created. Suddenly, where once there was a beautiful and peaceful Oneness, there was now a multitude of entities. Where there was perfect order, there was now chaos. What was whole was now shattered into infinite pieces.

Many of these pieces developed egos in order to know themselves as separate beings. And, once egos were created, competition began because they determined that they wanted to be different from one another. They decided they wanted to be bigger, stronger, smarter, better, richer, faster, healthier, louder, etc. The memory of the peaceful oneness became buried quickly in the rush to be counted as individuals. The reality that everyone and everything comes from the same whole only remained as a distant memory, if at all.

Regardless of the lengths our egos have gone in order to make us feel separate, we are not. Our separation from one another is only a myth, an illusion. The Big Bang may have put more space between all of our particles, but we are all still one. We are all made up of the same stuff. We are connected. *Period.*

Did you know that physics tells us there is actually more space between the particles of a solid object than we realize? Our senses tell us that our desks are solid. When we put our hands on our desks they don't feel like there is a lot of space. But science has proven that there is really more space than solid particle. There is more space than solid particles in the desk, the chair, the wall, the book, the pencil, etc. Science has proven this. But our senses deceive us.

So if our senses can deceive us about the desk being solid, why isn't it equally possible for us to be deceived about our separation?

Now, if our brains are telling us that what we are reading is false, it is because our egos desperately want to continue the illusion. They don't want us to learn their game. They will give us a thousand reasons why we really are different from our neighbor, our uncle, our teacher, our sister, the stranger asking for money, the politician on television, the professional athlete, the chef at our favorite restaurant, etc. Separation is vitally important to the ego because without it, it does not exist.

That's right. The illusion of separation is perpetuated so the ego can continue to tell us that we are different and more special than anyone else. It doesn't want us to see how we are similar to any of the people mentioned above.

Our egos can be a bit like the wicked witch in *The Wizard of Oz*. They don't want us to realize the truth. They don't want us to know how easy it is to go home. They like power and prefer to stay in control. And, just like Dorothy, we don't realize this. We become trapped in the tower of the ego's castle, away from our loved ones. We feel disconnected, with deep longing to go home, back to our oneness.

In the movie, Dorothy was moved by compassion to help her friend, Scarecrow. His straw arm was burning, and Dorothy wanted to help. She empathically felt his pain and wanted to stop it. Simple enough. She grabbed a bucket of water and tossed it in his direction. And that's when the magic happened. The witch was also splashed by the water, and the result was devastating to her.

While Scarecrow was saved by Dorothy's compassion and quick thinking, the witch started making a terrible noise and said, "I'm melting, melting. Ohhhhh, what a world; what a world. Who would have thought that some little girl like you could destroy my beautiful wickedness?"

She then literally melted into a big puddle on the floor, never to torture little dogs and tin men again.

Hah! That's a great moment in cinematic history and a wonderful illustration. We too, can toss the water of compassion and love on our egos. We can tell them that we no longer want to be separated from the oneness. They can either join us on our journey or melt into a big puddle on the floor. Either way, we can go back to our origins. We can click our heels three times and say, "There's no place like home." We can return to the One.

*_*_*_*_*_*_*_*

I am One with all that is
Eternally One
Infinitely One
Beyond the illusion of separation
With no room for time
And no instant of space
Only the One
The whole
The now

*_*_*_*_*_*_*_*

Once upon a time, in a land not so different than ours, there lived a leaf. This leaf fancied itself to be better than all the other leaves on the tree. It liked its shade of green more than any other shade of green. It liked its shape better than any other shape. And it liked its size a great deal as well.

As often as possible, this leaf told all the other leaves on the tree that it was better than they were. And in so many ways, it tried to prove to them that it was prettier and stronger and bigger and smarter and… well, you get the idea.

When a mighty wind came and blew the tree, and all the leaves bent together to help the branches from breaking, this leaf would not bend. It forced itself to stay straight so it could prove to the other leaves how strong and independent it was.

When the sun shined on the tree, and all the leaves used the light to make food to feed the tree, this leaf would rest in the shade. It wanted the other leaves to see that it didn't have to help out because it was special.

When the rain came and all the leaves let the raindrops fall from their tips to the ground so the roots could absorb the water and nourish the entire tree, this leaf kept the water for itself. It didn't feel the need to share with anyone.

Now, this tree and most of its leaves were very kind and allowing. They listened when *the* leaf boasted about itself. They did not criticize or reprimand. They just continued to dance in the wind and drink in the sun and bathe in the rain with joy.

One day, a man walked down the path by the tree and stopped to admire it. It was indeed a beautiful tree, and a slight breeze blew the leaves, as if to show the man just how wonderfully it could sway. But one leaf in particular stood out. When the breeze blew, the "special" leaf (as it often referred to itself) did not move, and this caught the man's attention. He decided that he wanted to remember this beautiful tree for a long, long time, and he plucked the special leaf from the tree and put it in his pocket.

Well, the leaf was in heaven. It knew without a doubt that it was different because, out of all the leaves on the tree, the man picked it. It *must* be better than all the others. It felt truly remarkable...

But the man's pocket was cramped and dark. The leaf couldn't feel the wind or the sun. And later, when it was tossed on a table in the man's room, it realized it wasn't quite so green anymore. And it was so hot and dry in the room. And there was a coin holding it down. And the man was busy doing other things and paid the leaf no attention at all.

Thankfully, the next day the man smiled, picked up the leaf, and held it up in the air, spinning it between his fingers. Again the leaf felt happy. The leaf tingled with excitement while the man walked across the room to a bookshelf and pulled out a big book. He opened the book, placed the leaf carefully on a page, and slammed the book closed. He then placed the book back on the shelf.

Outside, the sun was shining on the beautiful tree, and the breeze caressed the remaining leaves as they danced joyfully. They were happy because they never forgot that they were part of the tree. Seeing themselves as separate or different wasn't beneficial at all. The tree helped feed them and keep them grounded. And together they weathered storms and made a wonderful musical sound when the wind blew. They were connected in a perfect way, and this made them happy and content!

We are like these leaves, all connected to a tree that grounds and nourishes us. It helps us bend in the wind and drink in the sun as the branches reach to the sky. We are blessed to be part of the tree. Let's remember to honor each other and the tree each day and not get lost in our "specialness" or individuality. Make friends with a stranger. Call an old friend. Smile at someone on the checkout line.

After all, we are all in this tree together.

CHAPTER THREE

WHAT IS WHOLARIAN?

Upon the conduct of each depends the fate of all.
—Alexander the Great

To thine own self be true, and it must follow, as the night the day,
thou canst not then be false to any man.
—William Shakespeare

Whenever you do a thing, act as if all the world were watching.
—Thomas Jefferson

THREE

Whol-ar-i-an (hohl-**air**-ee-*uh*n)
n—One who is concerned with or believes in a complete, entire
wholeness of being and connection to oneness
adj—incorporating the concept of oneness in theory or practice

*_*_*_*_*_*_*

To be Wholarian is to know that we are One with everything, with no exceptions. It is to grasp that we are part of the whole, which encompasses all that we can and cannot see. It is appreciating that we are part of a team, and no one truly "wins" unless and until all the team members cross the finish line. It is about connecting with others, connecting with the world, and connecting with ourselves.

It is not a religion. It is not a political party. It is not a club and it doesn't abide by man-made laws, rules, or regulations.

To experience Wholarian Vision means seeing others without prejudice or bias. We aren't concerned with divisions or geographic boundaries. There is no us or them. It is simply the whole—the One.

And all these ideas apply not only to our fellow human beings, but to the land, sea, sky, and air, and everything that resides there. It reaches out to the farthest reaches of the heavens and down into the core of everything there is.

For those who might think or feel that this concept is disempowering because we will lose our individual identity, please know that nothing can be further from the truth. Each individual is necessary to the whole.

Each piece of the jigsaw puzzle is required to complete the picture. Every unique talent or quality is essential to the task. You and your "you-ness" are a vital part of the One. You are not optional.

A shattered vase cannot be reassembled until all the parts are found and placed back where they belong. From the biggest shards to the tiniest sliver, the vase is incomplete unless all the pieces are there. Even a seemingly insignificant missing piece can cause the vase to leak, the pattern to be incomplete, or the shape to be irregular. Each and every piece is significant, just as each and every one of us is significant.

When we realize that we are Wholarian, we understand that what we do to ourselves we also do to the whole. No choice we make is made in a vacuum. Each word we speak, each dollar we spend, each action we take touches the whole in some way. Thus, the concept of integrity is key. The word integrity stems from the Latin word *integer,* which means whole and complete. The dictionary states that integrity is the quality or state of being complete or undivided. A synonym for integrity is completeness. When we live in integrity, what we do is in alignment with ourselves as well as the whole.

Integrity is often associated with ethics and values. This makes perfect sense. When we have high standards of ethics and values, we choose to act in a way that does not harm others. Our behavior is adjusted so that we keep a higher purpose and greater good in mind. We subconsciously remember our connection to those around us and make choices that benefit the group. After all, we do share the same planet and drink the same water. We breathe the same air and look at the same stars.

If you have the opportunity, I suggest you read a beautiful children's book published in 1994 by Chara M. Curtis. It is entitled *All I See is Part of Me.* Here is a quick excerpt:

> "Sister Star, how can it be
> That I am you and you are me?"
>
> She glowed, "You're larger than you know,
> You are everyplace there is to go.
> You have a body, this is true...
> But look at what's inside of you!"

In this book, a young boy discovers his inner light and the light in everything around him. It is a celebration of life's interconnectedness and the concept of oneness. The little boy is essentially learning that he is Wholarian, although the word did not exist when the book was written. There is a lesson here for children and adults alike.

I also encourage you to look at examples of a Wholarian world in nature. YouTube is filled with videos of animals from different species that befriend each other. Stories of a dog and an elephant, a bird and a cat, a hippo and a tortoise all show us how to truly bond. Besides watching videos, we can walk in the woods and see how different plants and animals benefit from one another. There exists an extraordinary balance in the web of life that can become disrupted if one part is tugged too hard or destroyed. We have much to learn about living together in unity from the earth and all its inhabitants.

*_*_*_*_*_*

My heart is so full
That now it's no longer my heart
It encompasses all of me
All of who I am
And all that I see
My heart beats to the pulse of the universe
Everything is a cell in my body
And I am a cell in all that surrounds me
Everything is One
And One is everything
And with the knowing
We can all be

*_*_*_*_*_*_*

In March 2008, an amazing story out of New Zealand hit many newspapers around the world. A Pygmy whale and her calf were stranded on a sandbar and unable to find their way back out to sea. Humans attempted to help the whales, but after four attempts to lift them off the sandbar, the whales and the humans were getting tired and cold. Conversations were started about euthanizing the whales to keep them from suffering.

But, an unlikely hero appeared on the scene and saved the day. A female dolphin, named Moko by the locals, called to the whales. And amazingly, they returned her calls. The whales then followed Moko on a path parallel to the beach for about two hundred yards, at which point they made a right turn out to sea. They have not been seen since. Moko, on the other hand, continues to entertain bathers in that region.

Who knew that dolphins and whales could communicate with one another? Did Moko know that the whales were in danger? Did the whales know that Moko would help them out to sea? With this as an example, there are probably far more interspecies communications than we know.

*_*_*_*_*_*_*_*

I lay down and closed my eyes in the middle of the woods on a beautiful, hot summer day. With a quiet mind and a full heart, I waited to hear the song. Flies zoomed high, and the breeze whispered low. Tree limbs tapped together with an irregular rhythm. And bird songs brought a melody to it all. While I listened patiently and contentedly to the music of the woods, I felt a tickle on my knee. I barely opened one eye to see what could be causing the sensation. Much to my delight I noticed the very beginning of a spider's web forming. How honored I felt that a spider had chosen me as a worthy anchor for its palace. Unfortunately, my new friend and impromptu architect vanished as quickly as it had come. But it left a message that was quite clear. I too am an intricate part of the web of life. I am part of the song in the woods. Upon this realization, I began to hum a melody that seemed familiar, but from so long ago. It came from deep in my cells, and it blended in the most wonderful way with the serenade I had been enjoying. Oh, what a blessing to be part of the music of the woods.

*_*_*_*_*_*_*_*

I sat alone on a big rock in the middle of a field as two young girls walked toward me. When they reached the rock, the smaller, more animated girl climbed up without a moment of hesitation or concern. Even though we had never met before, she sat right beside me, introduced herself as Amanda, and asked me to tell her a story. I loved her boldness and lack of inhibition. It was so wonderfully refreshing. On a hunch, I told her I would gladly tell her a story, but I was wondering if she had a story to tell me. Her head bobbed up and down enthusiastically, and she then told me the following story:

"There once was a rabbit… ummm… a rabbit and a horse. Yes… a rabbit and a horse got together in a field near a big rock. And then came lots and lots and lots of people and other animals too, like birds and deer and squirrels and more rabbits and horses. They were all near the big rock and they were all dancing together!"

I asked, "Why were they dancing, Amanda?"

She shrugged her little shoulders, looked me in the eyes, and said, "Because they remembered. They remembered that they were all friends before. They all knew each other a long time ago. They remembered… and that's why they were dancing."

I smiled and said that her story was the best I had ever heard. She giggled a wonderful five-year-old's giggle that made my heart melt.

We talked for a little while longer before her family approached and said that they had to go. She scrambled down the rock, took her older sister's hand, and started to walk away.

But she turned her head one last time to say to me, "Just remember, nothing is impossible." With that she skipped away.

Amanda's beautiful spirit and her loving message live on in my heart. If I ever meet her again, I will ask her to dance with me around the big rock in the field as we remember that we were friends a long time ago. And chances are it will happen. After all, nothing is impossible.

SECTION TWO

MIND, BODY, SPIRIT

AFFIRM

—Ella Wheeler Wilcox (1850–1919)

Body and mind, and spirit, all combine
To make the Creature, human and divine.

Of this great trinity no part deny.
Affirm, affirm, the Great Eternal I.

Affirm the body, beautiful and whole,
The earth-expression of immortal soul.

Affirm the mind, the messenger of the hour,
To speed between thee and the source of power.

Affirm the spirit, the Eternal I—
Of this great trinity no part deny.

CHAPTER FOUR

THE WHOLARIAN MIND

To enjoy good health, to bring true happiness to one's family, to bring peace to all, one must first discipline and control one's own mind. If a man can control his mind he can find the way to Enlightenment, and all wisdom and virtue will naturally come to him.
—Buddha

He who knows nothing is closer to the truth than he whose mind is filled with falsehoods and errors.
—Thomas Jefferson

Meditation gives you an opportunity to come to know your invisible self. It allows you to empty yourself of the endless hyperactivity of your mind, and to attain calmness. It teaches you to be peaceful, to remove stress, to receive answers where confusion previously reigned.
—Dr. Wayne W. Dyer

FOUR

Neurotheology is the study of the biological basis of spirituality. And scientists use neuroimaging to pinpoint the brain regions that are activated during experiences that subjects associate with "spiritual" feelings or images. In a *Newsweek* article (May 7, 2001) entitled "Religion and the Brain," Sharon Begley writes about an experiment in which brains were monitored during deep meditation. Dr. Michael J. Baime offered his brain to the study, along with seven Tibetan Buddhists, all of whom were skilled meditators.

The experiment consisted of the subjects entering deep meditation. In the article, Dr. Baime describes the feeling of peak transcendence during his meditation this way:

"There was a feeling of energy centered within me... going out to infinite space and returning... There was a relaxing of the dualistic mind, and an intense feeling of love. I felt a profound letting go of the boundaries around me, and a connection with some kind of energy and state of being that had a quality of clarity, transparency, and joy. I felt a deep and profound sense of connection to everything, recognizing that there never was a true separation at all."

Once the subjects reached this level of transcendence, they signaled the waiting neurologists, and a radioactive tracer was injected into an IV line in their arms. Then a SPECT (Single Photon Emission Computed Tomography) machine was used to monitor the activity of the brain.

It was no surprise that the prefrontal cortex showed heightened activity. This part of the brain is linked to concentration, and meditation often utilizes forms of concentration. What was interesting was the part of the brain that got "quiet" and showed no activity. "A bundle of neurons in the superior parietal lobe toward the top and back of the brain had gone dark. This region, nicknamed the 'orientation association area,' processes information about space and time, and the orientation of the body in space. It creates the sensation of a physically delimited body; the right orientation area creates the sense of the physical body in space."

It was determined that since meditation essentially blocked off communication to this area of the brain, "Meditators feel as if they have touched infinity." They reached a state known as self-transcendence, which means going beyond the state of separation by decreasing the sense of self, hence identifying with the universe as a whole. This phenomenon is no longer considered just a spiritual experience. It is actually being monitored through scientific experiments as an observable fact. Several other studies have been done since the one mentioned in *Newsweek,* and all have reached the same conclusion. There is a part of the brain that is directly responsible for allowing us to feel connected to the universe.

Since it has been determined that the brain can help us reach this place of self-transcendence, it would help to know how to achieve this state. Quieting the part of the mind that holds on dearly to a separate identity can be accomplished one of two ways.

The first is, unfortunately, obtained through damage to the brain by lesions, injury, or surgery. Obviously, this is not a preferred method. And the second way is through meditation, or getting beyond our "thinking" mind into a deeper state of relaxation or awareness.

Meditation has been practiced throughout the centuries and is recognized by all the major religions as an acceptable and encouraged discipline. By quieting our own thinking and becoming less invested in our separate identity, we are able to more readily receive spiritual guidance and inspiration. And now we see that it also frees us from the constraints of individualism and allows us to commune with all that is. Suffice it to say, there are many, many different types of meditation practices. A case can be made for the effectiveness of each. However, the question of which type of meditation you practice is far less important than the question of whether or not you meditate.

Ask anyone who meditates regularly, and he will tell you what a difference it makes in his life. And now science is proving that meditation not only makes you feel better mentally, it can positively affect your overall health. There is an entire page dedicated to meditation on the Mayo Clinic's website. Here is the Mayo Clinic's description of meditation:

"Meditation can give you a sense of calm, peace, and balance that benefits both your emotional well-being and your overall health. And these benefits don't end when your meditation session ends. Meditation can help carry you more calmly through your day and improve certain medical conditions."

The web page goes on to list the following emotional benefits:

- Gaining a new perspective on stressful situations
- Building skills to manage your stress
- Increased self-awareness
- Focusing on the present
- Reducing negative emotions

And they list the following conditions meditation may benefit:

- Allergies
- Anxiety disorders
- Asthma
- Binge eating
- Cancer
- Depression
- Fatigue
- Heart disease
- High blood pressure
- Pain
- Sleep problems
- Substance abuse

Additionally, they give the following advice:

"Be sure to talk to your health care provider about the pros and cons of using meditation if you have any of these or other medical conditions.

Meditation isn't a replacement for traditional medical treatment. But it can be useful in addition to your other treatment."

So what do you have to lose? Meditation is free. It doesn't take much time. Just ten to fifteen minutes each day can have an impact. And look at all the benefits! It's been practiced for thousands of years, so there is obviously something to it. And it brings you much closer to the Wholarian mind of Oneness.

In addition, minding our thoughts is another important step toward achieving the Wholarian mind. It is no accident that happy people generally live longer, healthier lives. Studies are proving it. Those who think positive, empowering thoughts have a better quality of life. And there really is no wiggle room here. If we dwell in negative thoughts, negative things happen. If we are angry people, we tend to attract and awaken anger in others. If we are nervous, we tend to make the people around us jumpy too.

And likewise, when we walk into a room with a smile, we make others feel happier and lighter. When we keep a healthy sense of humor about life, we notice that even difficult situations go more smoothly. And thinking and believing that the best will happen means that, for us, it usually does.

So, our thoughts not only have a direct effect on our lives but also on the lives of those around us. Break the negative, self-deprecating-thought habit. Move away from the endless loops of worry, anger, mistrust, etc. Move toward the habit of seeing things as beautiful, fun, extraordinary, and even miraculous. See what a difference it makes.

*_*_*_*_*_*_*_*_*

A musician hears a few notes in her head. She writes them down. Perhaps she plays them on an instrument or sings them. If she likes them enough, she may add other parts that can be played by other musicians. Those musicians may play together for an audience, and the song may be recorded. This recording is then heard by hundreds or thousands or millions of people. Radio stations play the song, and it travels invisibly through the air as waves through our atmosphere. People sing and dance along to the melody. Student orchestras may play the song. People may call it their wedding song. It may become the music that plays when your phone call is put on hold. And to think, it all started as a note in a musician's head...

*_*_*_*_*_*_*_*

I think of you
And you are here with me
I see you as clearly
As the last time
We walked together
You never really left
Because I remember you
As perfectly, as clearly
As the last time we walked together

*_*_*_*_*_*_*_*

She closed her eyes as she sat cross-legged on the warm, flat stone next to the pond. The buzz of dragonflies could be heard flying through the air, as well as the scamper of chipmunks in the fallen leaves. Trish felt an itch on her foot, but she resisted the urge to scratch it. More than anything, she wanted to relax and put her newly found love of meditation into practice.

Trish had been through some tough times lately. She was promoted at work, which is definitely a good thing. However, she was now spending a lot more time behind a desk with much more responsibility. Then there was the sudden break-up of her five-year relationship when she discovered that her boyfriend was cheating on her with a good friend. This left her feeling betrayed by two important people in her life. And finally, she had to move out of the house she shared with her boyfriend because it was his. Altogether, the new job, the end of her relationship, as well as an unexpected move led to some stressful moments.

Friends began to worry because Trish lost a lot of weight. And she was having trouble sleeping. But she really knew it was time to grab her life back after she ran a stop sign that she never saw. Thankfully, no one was hurt when she hit the other car. And although it was an unfortunate accident, it was the wake-up call Trish needed to make some changes.

In the office building where she worked was a gym with lots of signs advertising yoga classes. She passed the signs often and had not paid attention before. Then, the day after her accident, a coworker asked Trish if she would like to sign up for a yoga class. The coworker had never done it before and was nervous. Trish realized this would be a good chance to try something new. The next day, they went to the gym and signed up for a class together.

If nothing else, Trish enjoyed the fact that she could get out of her suit and heels and put on comfortable yoga clothes. She wasn't sure what to expect from the class, but she already felt more relaxed. Then she was instructed to take a mat and wait for the class to begin. Trish and her coworker unrolled their mats and sat together talking for a few minutes.

This particular class was called Iyengar Yoga, for beginners. And the gentleman who was teaching the class was named Jeff. When he walked into the room, he immediately noticed a few new faces and informed everyone that he would explain everything thoroughly so no one would feel lost. He seemed peaceful and soft-spoken, which made Trish feel less nervous. He told them that the different postures were called "asanas," and he would demonstrate each one before they tried it.

As he named each asana, Trish smiled because they were in a foreign language and sounded exotic. She listened closely to Jeff's descriptions and then watched as he demonstrated each posture. He made them look easier than they were. Trish wasn't able to make her body do everything she was seeing, but Jeff was reassuring and showed everyone in the class how a little shift could make the whole posture work better. Even though she felt awkward, Trish was enjoying the movement of her body.

After about forty-five minutes, Jeff told all the students to lie down on their mats with arms at their sides and legs straight. At first, Trish thought this was the easiest asana yet, but then she realize something else was happening when Jeff dimmed the lights and asked everyone to inhale deeply, hold the breath a moment, and then exhale. The next ten minutes felt like a dream to Trish. Jeff instructed them to focus on their breathing and let go of any stray thoughts that popped into their heads, as if they were letting go of helium balloons into the sky. She had never meditated before, and this was love at first breath. That night, Trish slept better than she had in a long time.

After that first class, Trish continued attending as often as her schedule allowed. There were several instructors who had slightly different styles. Each class was a little different, so she never got bored. And she found that both the physical exercise and the calming meditation were helping her feel better and more centered. She even found herself occasionally closing her office door at work for a few minutes to take some deep breaths and meditate. Gradually, her appetite returned, and she began to feel healthier overall.

Her love for meditation grew over the next few months. And when an opportunity came up to rent a cabin in the woods for a week, she jumped at it. She was looking forward to getting away from the hustle and bustle for a while and meditating in the woods without distractions. This was going to be a little slice of paradise.

So, when Trish finally sat cross-legged on the warm flat stone next to the pond, she immediately started her conscious breathing exercise and felt a deep sense of peace envelop her. The soft breeze and the sounds of the woods just became part of her meditation…

She wasn't sure how long she was there. When Trish meditated, she felt like she was in a place that was timeless. It could have been twenty minutes or two hours when she slowly began to open her eyes and look around. The trees seemed so green, and the sky was very blue. And the pond was so still she could clearly see her reflection. She could even see the smile on her face. The other thing she saw was a beautiful reflection right beside her, only a few feet away. It was a doe and her baby. They had approached so quietly that Trish hadn't heard them. The fawn drank silently as the doe looked around for signs of danger. Once the baby had its fill and the mother took a quick drink, they slowly walked back into the woods.

Once they were far enough away, Trish sighed deeply. Wild animals don't usually bring their young near humans. She knew she must have meditated into such a state of deep peace that the doe did not fear her. Trish's heart became full with gratitude and happiness as she thought about how far she had transformed her life in only a couple of months. The presence of the doe and the fawn confirmed for her that she was on the right path now.

After a few more deep breaths, Trish stretched her legs, stood up, and headed back to the cabin. She sat down to eat some cool, refreshing watermelon and knew she would never forget this day by the pond as long as she lived.

CHAPTER FIVE

THE WHOLARIAN BODY

To keep the body in good health is a duty... otherwise we shall not be able to keep our mind strong and clear.
—Buddha

Our bodies are our gardens—our wills are our gardeners.
—William Shakespeare

Healing is a thought by which two minds perceive their oneness and become glad.
—A Course in Miracles

FIVE

An adult body is a close-knit community of about fifty trillion cells working miraculously in relative harmony throughout its lifetime. And the things it does is truly quite extraordinary. On average, the human brain has about one hundred billion nerve cells that can send impulses at a speed of anywhere from 1 to 120 meters per second. The heart pumps about 1 million barrels of blood during an average lifetime—that's enough to fill more than three super tankers. And your body has about 5.6 liters (six quarts) of blood that circulate through the body three times every minute. In one day, the blood travels a total of 19,000 km (12,000 miles)—that's four times the distance across the United States from coast to coast. But, the truth is, we take all this for granted and don't treat our bodies with the respect they deserve.

We eat foods that aren't always nutritious
and drink beverages that are quite suspicious.
We breathe air that isn't very good
and exercise less than we should.
We're working way too many hours
and forget to smell the pretty flowers.
Our sleeping hours are quite few
and when we eat, we hardly chew.
Our favorite seat is a comfy couch
that causes our weakened backs to slouch.
And if we stop to check our weight
we don't always feel so great.

This list is getting rather long,
but the point it makes is strong.

We owe it to our fifty trillion cells to pay more attention and take better care. Don't you think? When we do, it serves a few purposes. Remember that our health or our illness has a ripple effect on the rest of the world. Consider this. Neglecting ourselves causes challenges that are experienced beyond our body. In one example, poor eating habits can lead to heart disease, diabetes, obesity, etc. This then creates a burden on families, the health-care system, and society. Surplus medicines are found in our water supply. Children are finding prescriptions in the medicine cabinets and being poisoned by drugs.

On the other side of the scale, when we take care of our bodies, it has a positive ripple effect:

Healthy Self → Healthy Family → Healthy Community → Healthy Society → Healthy Planet

Here's an easy suggestion for one healthy meal each day. Do you have a blender? If not, buy one. It needs to be a good one that can really break down food, not just mix cocktails. Now, buy some fresh, ripe, organic bananas, organic blueberries, an organic pear, and about two cups of fresh organic spinach or kale. That's right… spinach or kale. Do *not* skip this ingredient. And please make sure that you buy all organic fruits and vegetables. Also, wash everything well.

Now, peel two bananas and put them in the blender. Add one cup of blueberries. Core the pear and cut it up. Throw that in the blender too. Get ready, because it's time for the well-washed spinach or kale to go in. Don't be afraid! After your greens are in, add two to three cups of filtered water and put the lid on. Okay, turn it on and watch it blend. Let it get "smoothified" at high speed for about one minute. Turn it off and pour yourself a glass.

Take a sip… Hold it in your mouth for a minute. Swish it around. Now swallow.

Are you surprised? It tastes amazing, and it is so good for you. And think how many servings of fruits and vegetables you got in one sitting. The best part is that it's delicious.

Can you make one of these every morning for breakfast? You can see that it doesn't take very long. If you are crunched for time in the morning, make it the night before and keep it in the fridge.

Now, here's your challenge. Have one of these every day for one week. If that isn't too difficult, increase it to two weeks. And for those who absolutely love it, go for twenty-one days and beyond, as research shows that you can develop a new habit in twenty-one days. This is the ultimate. You will feel such a difference when you drink these green smoothies on a regular basis.

Green smoothies are good and good for you. They help you easily increase your fiber intake. They give you several helpings of fruits and vegetables. And they are in a form that is easy for the body to assimilate. What does that mean? It means that if I put the bananas, pear, blueberries, and spinach or kale on your plate and asked you to eat it, you would have a hard time eating it all in one sitting, for starters. Also, you would only chew each mouthful a few times before swallowing, so you wouldn't get all of the nutritional value from it. And if you've ever tried to eat raw kale, you know that it is just really tough.

You can see that improving your eating habits is easy and tastes good too. Here are some other simple suggestions for improving your overall health:

- Drink more water and use a water filter for your drinking water and your shower
- Use an air filter, especially in rooms where you spend a lot of time (bedroom, office, etc.)
- Use no/low VOC paint when painting
- Buy and eat plenty of organic fruits and vegetables
- Share a dessert instead of eating the whole thing yourself
- Cut down on processed foods (hint: if you don't know what it originally looked like, it's processed)
- Sit down, eat slowly, and thoroughly chew your food at every meal
- Park a distance away from your destination and walk a few extra steps
- Bike to your destination if you can
- Exercise 10–15 minutes per day

- Use natural body care products—many additives are found to have negative, long-term health effects
- Relax
- Meditate fifteen minutes every day
- Spend time with friends, family and loved ones—social connections are a key to good health

As a matter of fact, strong social ties have a number of health benefits. Loving relationships have been shown by many studies to protect the heart and increase lifespan. It is also possible that they may help cut dementia risk and reduce stress. And, it seems that people who are more social also have more robust immune systems.

Since we are connected to all that is around us, by taking care of ourselves and our physical bodies, we are helping to take care of the world.

*_*_*_*_*_*_*_*

Early morning
My toes touch the ground
A soft cotton mat beneath my feet
Almost as soft as the edges on my still sleepy mind
Slowly get up and walk
Until my bare feet touch the cool tile floor
Moving the soft edges over a bit
Into the realm of substance
Thoughts becoming more concrete
Then over the edge of the tub
Into the warm shower water
Washing away the last of the fuzzy dreams
That clung around and around and around
And down the drain along with the sleep from my eyes
As I dry my face and body with a towel
And put on shoes which will keep me in line
Throughout the day
Until I can take my shoes off again
And dream

*_*_*_*_*_*_*

I had a dream one night that I met a person I didn't like very much. She was someone I had never met in person, but I was made aware of some of her activities, and they upset me considerably. So, in the dream I wanted to talk to her about why she had done these things. As I approached her, I realized she was my height and approximately my weight. She had my hair color and eye color and spoke just like me. I knew in real life these things weren't true, but in the dream we were the mirror image of one another. Then it struck me that we were far more alike than not, both in reality and in the dream. And even though I didn't agree with her actions, she was a human being going through life the best way she knew how, just like me. We were in separate bodies, but we were so much the same.

I woke up feeling compassion for her. I didn't have to agree with the things she had done in order to see her as a fellow human. I didn't have to like the things she did in order to like her.

*_*_*_*_*_*_*

Jason was the shortest and skinniest boy in his class. He looked about one or two years younger than he actually was. And in fifth grade, that can make a big difference. Some of the other kids in his class made fun of him and called him Shorty or Peanut, which upset Jason quite a bit. He didn't like to feel different; he just wanted to look like everyone else. Because he felt like an outcast, Jason kept to himself and didn't play much with the other kids. Instead, he read a lot of books and loved learning about geology. Rocks and fossils were fascinating to him, and he had quite a nice collection in his bedroom.

One day in school, the teacher announced a field trip to a nearby park. The class cheered with excitement. They would be able to run around in the field, play games, spend time on the large playground with swings and slides, play ball, and eat a special bag lunch. But Jason didn't care about those things at all. The kids never included him in their games anyway. He was excited too because he knew there was a small cave at the park he could explore. He had explored it once before with his father. Jason figured no one would miss him if he spent some time there. So, along with the other children, he eagerly took the permission slip home that evening to be signed by his parents and returned it the next day with a smile on his face.

The trip was two weeks away, but every day the classroom was buzzing with anticipation. Everyone talked about what snacks to bring, what games they would play, how fun the bus ride was going to be, and so many other things. They also kept looking out the window at the rain and hoped that they would have a sunny day for their trip. This had been a particularly soggy spring, and if it rained the day of the trip, it would be cancelled. No one wanted to think about that.

Luckily, the afternoon before the field trip, the skies cleared and the weatherman predicted beautiful weather for a few days. Sure enough, the sun was shining brightly on the morning of the trip as everyone climbed onto the bus to go to the park. While all the children talked loudly and excitedly on the bus ride, Jason took a window seat and watched the sights roll by. All he could think about was looking for new rocks to add to his collection. He was sure the cave held some special treasures. A few of the boys in the class were trying to pick on Jason and called him Peanut. But he was in a good mood and ignored them. This seemed to bother the boys even more, but Jason didn't care.

An hour or so later, the bus arrived at the park, and the children, teachers, and chaperones got off the bus. Jason knew he would have to plan his breakaway carefully because there were a lot of adults monitoring the group. So, he told one of the adults that he left his hat on the bus and needed to go back and get it. While he was doing that, a small fight broke out between a few of the kids, and the adults were distracted long enough for Jason to sneak in the other direction and run off toward the cave. He was thrilled about his little adventure and ran all the way without stopping.

Once he got to the cave, he pulled out the flashlight he kept in his backpack and entered the cave through the small entrance. Jason knew that he needed to watch his footing in the cave. Rocks can dislodge easily and without warning. So, he carefully walked forward as he shined the flashlight on the floor and looked for rocks to examine. He was concentrating deeply for a few minutes when he thought he heard something behind him. He turned to look and his stomach sank.

Three of the boys in his class had followed him to the cave. They were the same boys who always made fun of his small size and had been giving him a hard time on the bus that morning. Jason knew they weren't here to look for rocks, and he started to back away. The bigger boys laughed because the cave wasn't very big, and soon Jason's back was against the furthest wall.

They walked toward him, picking up rocks and saying loudly, "Can't get away from us this time, Shorty!"

But what happened next, no one expected. Because of all the rain over the past few weeks, the ground was saturated. The boys had been yelling loudly, kicking stones, brushing up against the walls of the cave when they heard some rumbling noises. Their vibrations had caused a small avalanche of rocks and debris. Within seconds, the entrance of the cave was sealed off, and all the boys were in the dark wondering what to do. Immediately they realized none of the teachers knew where they were because they had run to the cave without permission. They knew they could be trapped for a long time if they didn't get help. And one of the boys was hurt by the falling rocks and couldn't move his leg. He would need medical attention quickly.

Jason's flashlight still worked, and he looked at the faces of the other boys. Jason was the only one in the group who wasn't terrified. He had read in his spelunking books that panicking was the worst thing you could do in that situation. So he sat quietly for a few minutes and then shut the flashlight off. The other three boys started yelling at him again to turn the light back on. But Jason knew what he was doing. He waited for his eyes to adjust and then he saw what he was looking for. Above them, in the roof of the cave, there was some sunlight coming through. It was a small hole, but this was their only way out. Jason planned out what he needed to do, but he couldn't do it alone.

Jason showed the boys the hole, and they looked at him without understanding. They were confused. Jason explained that even though the hole wasn't very big, his body was the right size to go through it and get help. They would just need to lift him up to reach it. At first they were too scared to move, but when the boy with the hurt leg started to cry, the other two realized they had to do something quickly. So, they helped Jason stand on their shoulders, and he reached up and pulled himself through the hole. It was a very tight fit, and if he was any bigger, he would not have been able to get out. It took some wiggling, but Jason got his arms and shoulders through the hole and into the fresh air.

Once he pulled himself all the way up and had his feet on the ground, Jason ran back to find the adults and tell them what happened. He then ran back with the teacher and an adult to show them where the cave was. The other chaperones stayed behind and called for help. Within minutes, there were emergency vehicles on the scene. Because Jason had gotten some bumps and scrapes during the ordeal, he was taken to the hospital to be checked. So, he didn't see when the three boys were pulled out of the cave a few hours later. They were all scared and dirty but very happy to be alive.

Jason's doctor said he should take a few days off from school to recuperate. And while he was home, he had to promise his mother and father over and over that he would never enter a cave without telling them first. They were upset with him but also happy that he was relatively unhurt. His parents were also quite astonished that he had the presence of mind to get out of the cave so quickly to fetch help. His ability to stay calm saved him and the other boys that day. There was no doubt about that.

A few days later, Jason returned to school and was surprised to see his desk decorated with ribbons and bows. All the students ran up to him as he tried to take his seat. The teacher then asked everyone to give Jason room to breathe and explained what was happening. It seems that the boys who had been bullying Jason told the teacher everything that happened in the cave and how Jason saved their lives. They regretted making fun of Jason for his size and realized that if Jason had been any bigger, they may not have made it out of the cave that day. In other words, the very thing they had made fun of is exactly what saved them.

Suddenly, Jason didn't mind being so small. Being a peanut wasn't such a bad thing after all. It now was clear to him that he was exactly the way he was supposed to be. His small body was perfect, in this case. And when everyone had special cupcakes at snack time to celebrate, Jason showed them all that even a "shorty" can have a big appetite. He ate two cupcakes to prove it!

CHAPTER SIX

THE WHOLARIAN SPIRIT

I love you when you bow in your mosque, kneel in your temple, pray
in your church. For you and I are sons of one religion,
and it is the spirit.
—Kahlil Gibran

Humans are amphibians—half spirit and half animal. As spirits they
belong to the eternal world, but as animals they inhabit time.
—C. S. Lewis

If you want to accomplish the goals of your life,
you have to begin with the spirit.
—Oprah Winfrey

SIX

Spirit is the vital, yet intangible, essence of being. All that is living (and some would even argue, all that is not living) has a spirit. When we realize our Wholarian Spirit, we recognize that all spirit is connected and comes from a common source. With this awareness, we have an easier time seeing what we all have in common. When we are observing purely from a physical level, it is harder to do this.

We aren't generally taught how to get in touch with our spiritual essence. Especially in Western cultures, the fascination with the external often overshadows the desire to witness the internal. That quiet place within can be ignored for long stretches of time until it calls to us ever-so-softly and gently. Through peace, tranquility, serenity, and silence, we can find a connection with spirit.

I highly encourage everyone to find time to be quiet. As mentioned previously, meditation is one good way to do that. But there are other ways to consciously become more aware of our thoughts and actions and whether or not we are allowing ourselves to connect with spirit.

Personally, I was quite fortunate a few years ago to experience two weeks alone in a cottage on more than one hundred acres of wooded property in Massachusetts. There was no television, no radio, and no other human being for quite a distance. Talk about peace and quiet… that was in abundance on this retreat.

The amazing thing is that it really wasn't all that quiet out in the middle of the woods. There were all kinds of birdsongs to enjoy. Little critters were rustling around in the leaves under the trees. Chipmunks were chirping loudly at each other, at squirrels, and at the world. Insects were buzzing. The wind was blowing. There were many, many sounds to enjoy in the middle of the silence.

But perhaps the loudest noise of all was the one inside my head. It was going nonstop for the first few days. "What should I eat today?" "Which book should I read first?" "Should I take a walk now or later?" "Did I bring enough warm clothes?" "Did I bring the right shoes for hiking?" "Where is the nearest gas station?" "Did I bring enough food?" "How do I keep from getting a bug bite?" "Will I see a moose?" "Will I get poison ivy?" "Are there ticks here?"

Thankfully, after a few days of relaxation combined with a clear intention on my part to become quieter, and more connected, it began to happen. I watched silently as a hummingbird hovered in front of a window for a few minutes, its wings flapping so quickly they were just a blur. The pretty, bright green feathers made it look surreal. And it disappeared as quickly as it arrived.

And then there were the deer that walked out of the woods and into the clearing. They were enjoying eating the grass and kept a vigilant eye and ear out for anything that might disturb them. They grazed so peacefully at dusk until they decided to spring back into the woods.

I also saw a bear, a mole, hawks, turkeys, a wolf (or coyote, it was so dark I couldn't tell). I took long walks in the woods, spent hours reading and writing, caught up on my sleep, and took time just being peaceful.

On the days I ventured into town, I found myself feeling less like a participant in the world and more like an observer. Quieting my mind had given me a different perspective about the things I encountered. My actions felt more driven by spirit and less by ego. There was no sense of hurry or judgment. I didn't have a strong agenda, but more of a "whatever will be, will be" attitude. I found myself smiling more and rushing less.

And this beautiful sense of quietude and deep connection to spirit stayed with me well beyond my two weeks in the woods. While I was there, I experienced peace within myself. And once I had that peace, I viewed the world around me through more peaceful eyes. This in turn made everything seem more peaceful—and it was.

Perhaps you don't have two weeks to spend in the woods. Perhaps, you are saying, you don't even have two hours or two minutes to be peaceful. If that is the case, you owe it to yourself to find a way to turn off the news or get a babysitter for two hours or leave work a few hours earlier to make it happen. If you don't make it a priority, it won't occur. And that peacefulness is essential. Once you have your two minutes or more, use it to do things that lift your spirit. Walk in nature. Watch an uplifting movie. Read a positive book. Write some poetry. Paint a picture. Write a love letter. Make a phone call to someone you love. Pray. Sing a song. Take a few deep breaths. Prepare a nice meal. Take a bath by candlelight. And most of all, reconnect with spirit. It is as essential to nourish our spirits as it is to nourish our bodies.

Once we make time to connect with our spirit on a more regular basis, we realize we feel better about ourselves and those around us. We tend to have greater self-confidence and less anxiety. We are able to forgive more easily. We feel more gratitude. We appreciate little details more. Colors seem brighter and foods taste better. Life isn't as challenging. We sleep better. We breathe deeper. And we feel more connected to the One. We feel it inside us, outside us, and in everything we do.

*_*_*_*_*_*_*_*

My favorite meals as a child were any that included gravy. Gravy made *everything* taste better. It made the delicious foods taste even more delicious, and the foods I didn't enjoy… well, they became delightfully camouflaged. I was never a big eater, but the days we had gravy I would pile a little extra on my plate—even the foods I didn't like very much. Those boiled carrots were amazingly transformed once I put the brown sauce on them! And since a clean plate was the only option in our home, that gravy sure helped me with my picky eating habits.

Life is a lot like a dinner plate. Sometimes we are served things we love, and other times there are things put on our plate we don't like one bit. There are some days we get extra helpings of the tasty morsels, and other days where the boiled carrots and lima beans won't stop coming. And one way or another, we need to clean that plate. On those "lima bean kind of days," a dose of gratitude gravy helps a lot. It is the perfect food for body, mind, and spirit.

What exactly is gratitude gravy? And how do we make it? Well, the recipe looks something like this:

1 heaping cup of thanks for all the wonderful things in our lives
1 generous cup of appreciation for all the stuff that isn't in our lives
(which is a good thing)
A tablespoon of assorted spices that make us feel alive—
adjust to taste
As much fresh, living spirit as we can harvest
All the yummy drippings from our favorite memories

Place all the above ingredients in a pot over a very low heat and slowly stir with a heart full of love and joy until it is well blended and has a smooth texture. Once prepared, this recipe can be stored for a long time. Just remember to add more ingredients as they become depleted.

Serve gratitude gravy in generous portions over everything in your life. Be extra generous when times are difficult or unbearable. Share with others as often as possible.

Calories = 0 Carbohydrates = 0 Fats = 0
Heart Health = 100 percent Spirit Health = 100 percent

So the next time we end up with something on our plates (or in our lives) that seems sure to taste like an old smelly sock with Limburger cheese on it, grab the gratitude gravy and pour it on. Remember that the more thankful we are for the wonderful things in our lives, the less likely it is that the other things will even show up. And if they do, we now know what to do with them!

*_*_*_*_*_*_*_*_*

I stared at the wall in front of me
I stared and stared
And stared some more
Until my eyes burned and ached
But again I heard the voice say,
"Keep looking, child." And I did…

Until I saw it
At first I wasn't sure it was there
It was a blur, at best
So I blinked once, twice and looked again
And it was indeed there
The door
Waiting to be opened
Just waiting
Without a step I was in front of the door
With my fingers on the handle
I drew a breath
And held it...
Was it seconds or years that passed?
I'll never know for sure
But finally I moved the handle
The door opened smoothly
Into... into...
The place I always knew existed
But wasn't sure that I would see
What I saw before me was
Me
Here and Now
Eternally present
I walked through the door

The Labyrinth

It is evening and the labyrinth calls to you
"Just one more passage around," it says.
You don't ignore the call
You go back one more time
Flowing left, flowing right, slowly, peacefully
Filled with gratitude, filled with love
Placing your steps and being present
All the while the music of the universe is playing

Blending with your heartbeat and your breath
Making you quite light
And in the music there is a message of thanks
Emanating from the earth, the trees, the sky, the moon
This music of the universe meant for all to hear
It weaves itself around all that you see and can't see
Touching many hearts along the way
And you notice that you don't just hear this music in the sounds
You also hear it in the space between the sounds
It's not just in your footsteps
But in the pause between those steps
It is between your breaths
Between your heartbeats
And knowing this and feeling this you continue flowing
Slowly and peacefully until
You reach the center of the labyrinth
The center of the center
Where you stand still to just be
And you have been told that this is where the answer lies
At the stillness of the center
And that answer indeed comes to you
It is in the song you have been hearing
The song of gratitude is certainly for all to hear
But now, at the stillness of the center, you hear your name
The heavens, the earth, the stars, the trees
All call your name
And say
Thank you, thank you, thank you
Dear one, we send you an infinite and eternal
Thank you
For being part of the One

*_*_*_*_*_*_*

My friend and I leisurely strolled around the town of Rhinebeck in New York. There were so many nice shops to browse through and wonderful restaurants to eat in. It was a beautiful autumn day, and after looking around for a few hours, we decided to go to our next stop. We wanted to see the view of the Hudson River from Poet's Walk, as we had both heard so much about it. So, we started heading back toward the car to take the short drive north.

The fresh air and sunshine were intoxicating, making us laugh at everything we did. As we walked, we kicked a stone to see who could kick it farthest without knocking it off the sidewalk. We got it all the way to the parking lot when Jim saw a paper plate on the ground. We are both environmentally conscious people, so it didn't surprise me when he bent to pick it up. There was a garbage can close by, and I assumed Jim would simply toss it away.

But, being in a silly mood, Jim decided instead to fling it like a Frisbee. I laughed because it was so out of character for him to throw garbage around. What happened after that caught us both by surprise. The paper plate landed on its edge and began to roll. Since the parking lot was fairly empty, there was plenty of room for it to go freely on its way. However, it didn't just roll in a straight line. It actually began to dance. It twisted left and right, in circles and then straight, still on its edge and still rolling along. Perhaps it was the way the breeze was blowing. I wasn't sure. All I knew was that this paper plate was beautiful and captivating.

The paper plate dance went on for at least a full minute, maybe more. The plate seemed to be filled with spirit and grace. Jim and I kept looking at each other in disbelief. Then, with one last dramatic pirouette, the paper plate finally settled down. We both carefully walked up to it to see if there were strings attached or some other mechanism that may have cause this impromptu plate ballet. But now it looked like any other discarded piece of rubbish, complete with a few ketchup stains on it.

Jim quietly picked up the plate and placed it in the garbage can before we walked the final distance to the car. It took a few moments for us to say anything. After all, what do you say after you've seen something that defies logic? When we finally spoke, we both acknowledged that we had witnessed something special. We had just seen a paper plate dance.

SECTION THREE

WHOLARIAN WORLD

The universe has conspired to put you here. The totality of all the molecules and atoms that are floating around the universe, some of them temporarily gathering together and manifesting what looks like a person. They were forged in the furnace of stars and in this amazing way it's all coming together...
Everything is connected to everything else; it's all timeless.
—Eckhart Tolle

CHAPTER SEVEN

WHAT IS THE WHOLARIAN WORLD?

"All people are children, and of one family. The same tale sends them all to bed, and wakes them in the morning."
—Henry David Thoreau

"When one tugs at a single thing in nature, he finds it attached to the rest of the world."
—John Muir

"We cannot live only for ourselves. A thousand fibers connect us with our fellow men. "
—Herman Melville

SEVEN

Everyone around us is not only our neighbor but our friend, our relative, and our partner. That idea takes some getting used to, doesn't it? So many of us feel more comfortable being anonymous and not always making eye contact or saying hello to the people we pass on the street. Cutting ourselves off will not serve the bigger picture, however. But let's be clear. That doesn't mean we have to be social butterflies twenty-four hours a day, seven days a week, which is tiresome and unnecessary. It does mean we need to recognize our connections. We need to see the interconnectedness of all living beings in the world.

Recently, two amazing thing happened to bring us closer to this vision. On May 24, 2010, the New York State Assembly unanimously passed a nonbinding resolution stating that the United States and other nations must recognize humanity's underlying oneness for the sake of world peace. This may be the first resolution of its kind passed by US state lawmakers.

The resolution says:

"All people share the world together with all of life."

"Science has established, and sages have declared for millennia, that life is a unified whole with multiple dimensions and expressions."

It goes on to say that these multiple dimensions and expressions "complement each other and are an inherent part of life's underlying unity."

"It is of the utmost and urgent importance to the common interests of the entire state of New York, the United States of America, and the international community to strengthen the ideals of unity, diversity, harmony, and compassion within and among all nations and peoples," the resolution declared.

In addition, around the same time as the resolution was passed, the United Nations received a petition signed by more than fifty thousand people from 168 countries appealing to the world body to declare an annual global Oneness Day recognizing humanity's inner unity.

This is what a Wholarian World is all about. It is about recognizing our unity and declaring our Oneness. We are moving away from separatism. Think of the holiday cards that show people of all different nationalities holding hands around the circumference of the world. This is no longer a pipe dream. It is happening as we speak. On New Year's Day, we can see the fireworks from all different countries as they celebrate. The telecast usually starts in Sydney, Australia, and then progresses around the world. We can sit in front of our televisions or computers and watch as many different cultures observe the end of one year and the beginning of another. Sharing these common bonds helps unite us.

These days, there are so many things bringing the world closer. Televisions, cell phones, and the Internet are remarkable tools to help us communicate quickly with one another and see how similar we truly are. The Olympics and other sporting events bring people from different nations together. Music is often a unifying force. Even disasters have proven to bring people closer regardless of race, religion, gender, age, or language. Air travel allows us to be on the other side of the world in hours rather than weeks or months. And books are translated and printed in many languages so we can all read the words written in different countries with different perspectives.

And let's not forget the intangible, but no less important, unifying forces of love, compassion, faith, belief, and hope. Every culture, every religion, every country, every neighborhood, and every family share stories involving these feeling and emotions. Google the word "love" and get more than 4.2 billion results. That is how prevalent it is in our world and how important it is to all of us.

Besides human beings, the Wholarian World encompasses all living creatures. We are coming to realize the sad and tragic consequences of ignoring or, even worse, annihilating plants and animals in the name of progress. Extinction, pollution, disrupted ecosystems, landslides, famine, starvation, drought, etc. are often caused by myopic choices made by humans who lost sight (or just didn't care) about the relevance to the whole.

Some corrections are now being made. Many corrections are still being resisted. Ultimately, we need to realign with Gaia—our Mother Earth, in all her intricate beauty—if we want to leave an inhabitable future to our children and their children. We need to live in harmony with nature and not treat it as an enemy if we hope to be sustained for the long-term.

We are the caretakers. We are the ones on whom the future depends. We can choose to keep reusable shopping bags in our car, drink from glass or stainless steel water bottles instead of plastic, use recycled copy paper, wear clothing made of natural fibers, buy only non-aerosol sprays, drive higher MPG automobiles, etc. We can choose to look at the person on the street as our friend and neighbor. We can choose to eat more plant based, organic foods. We can choose to leave an inhabitable planet. The choice is ours. It is not too late to change our future, but we can't wait for someone else to do it. The time is now. The place is here. This is our Wholarian World.

*_*_*_*_*_*_*_*

When we think of going off into the woods to separate ourselves from society and the issues we may be experiencing, we often think of Henry David Thoreau, the author and poet. He's well known for building a small house in the woods and living there for two years. It was his experiment in simple living.

He picked a beautiful place to live. Walden Pond is surrounded by trees and nature at its finest. It is easy to see the appeal of such a tranquil place as an escape from society. He spent plenty of time writing while he was there.

But the truth is that Thoreau didn't really cut himself off from society at all. He lived close enough to town so he could walk there when needed. He entertained visitors at his cozy home and returned those visits. And, one of the funniest things is that he built his home near the railroad tracks. This way, when he wanted to visit his parents' home, which was 1.5 miles away, he could just follow the tracks and be there in a short amount of time. The image of Thoreau trudging home with his laundry on his back so his mother could do his wash seems humorous. She probably cooked him a few nice meal as well.

Oh well, so much for trying to separate from the rest of the world. Those connections are strong.

*_*_*_*_*_*_*_*_*_*

Some call us idealists
But through our eyes we see
That we can teach the world to sing
In perfect harmony

Some call us idealists
For in our hearts we know
That with some love and caring
World peace is sure to grow

Some call us idealists
But through our ears we hear
The songs of many peoples
And those songs are true and clear

We talk about a world of peace
And ask the question, *"How?"*
But there's only one right answer
And that answer's *here* and *now*

Come join us—the idealists—
And know the power of One
We'll have the peace we're looking for
When we're Wholarian

*_*_*_*_*_*_*

It was a perfect summer day for a walk through my favorite park. Caumsett has everything a park should have: paved and non-paved trails, a pond, a beach, a mansion, lots of wildlife, flowers, trees, a bird rehabilitation center, you name it. The only thing missing is a mountain, but it does have a really steep hill. That's the closest to a mountain you will get on the north shore of Long Island.

After a long work week, I was looking forward to exercise, fresh air, and time in nature. Nothing is more grounding to me than spending time in the woods, listening to the breeze, watching the squirrels and chipmunks scurry about, smelling the fallen leaves. Ahhh… just thinking about it was making me relax.

I had a short drive from my home to the park. The woman at the booth checked my pass, wrote down some numbers, and waved me on. Thankfully, there weren't too many cars in the lot, which meant I wouldn't have to worry about being run down by lots of enthusiastic bicycle riders.

My iPod was loaded with nice relaxing music. I was ready for the three mile loop and a meditation in the woods. As I walked, I counted the number of chipmunks that ran across the path. They were all over the place and not terribly afraid of people. Then there were the robins hopping about and the crows cawing from the trees. This was heaven. I felt so connected to all the living things around me.

When I got to the mansion, about halfway through the walk, I stopped at one of the side gardens to look for a place to sit quietly. I turned off the iPod and scouted out a place to relax. But as I got near a nice clearing, a little bird dove at me, chattering loudly. I instinctively covered my head, thinking it wanted to peck me for getting near its nest. It flew away, and I looked around but didn't see a tree or a shrub with a nest. Hmmm… that was odd.

As I began to look again, the bird came back and flew in my direction, making loud chirping noises. Again, I went into a defensive posture and looked around to see what I might be disturbing. But there was definitely no nest nearby. So when it came back a third time, I tried a different tactic.

When the little chickadee flew toward me the third time, I didn't flinch. I just gently lifted my finger into the air, and it landed there. I held my breath for fear of scaring it as I felt the little claws digging into my finger and its tiny heart beating rapidly. It looked at me for a few seconds, turned its head this way and that, and then flew away.

I exhaled and felt my own heart beating as fast as the little bird's. Had that really happened? Did that wild bird just land on my finger? Is that why it was trying to get my attention? Is that all it wanted?

The little bird didn't come back. I guess it needed a connection in that brief moment as much as I needed my connection to nature that day. I don't remember much about the rest of the walk. I just kept thinking about the trust of that chickadee and remembered the feeling of the claws on my finger and the tiny heartbeat that was in my hand for an instant.

CHAPTER EIGHT

WHOLARIAN RELATIONSHIPS

Spiritual relationship is far more precious than physical.
Physical relationship divorced from spiritual is body without soul.
—Mohandas Gandhi

Piglet sidled up to Pooh from behind. "Pooh!" he whispered. "Yes,
Piglet?" "Nothing," said Piglet, taking Pooh's paw.
"I just wanted to be sure of you."
—A.A. Milne

Am I not destroying my enemies when I make friends of them?
—Abraham Lincoln

EIGHT

If you turned to this chapter first, you would not be alone. As a society, we are fascinated by relationships and programmed at an early age to treasure certain relationships over others. Advertisers exploit this obsession. They tell us that our relationship with our partner, friends, family, and coworkers will all improve if we use their product. Better yet, many product promotions encourage us to think that if we purchase a particular item, we will suddenly find the relationship of our dreams.

Many books have been sold, because we are looking for those secret words that will make an existing relationship better or a perfect relationship instantly appear. Or maybe we want the instructions for a ritual that will attract the right partner. Or we desire explicit instructions for the "right" way to look, walk, dress, smell, talk, dance, drink, eat, etc. in order to be luckier in our romantic pursuit. Let's face it—as a society, we are addicted to love and the butterflies-in-the-stomach feeling we get when someone turns our head. And we are willing to do almost anything to get it.

But, the truth is, we have been misled, and we are going about it all wrong. One particular relationship is not the answer to our problems. One particular relationship will not cure our anger, fear, loneliness, shyness, or anxiety. One particular relationship will not even make us the coolest person on the planet.

Why? Because each individual relationship is a sum total of all our relationships, including our relationship with our authentic self. If we are bitter and resentful about someone from our past or present, those feelings will appear again with someone else. If we are happy, loving, and present in relationships, that will show up for us as well. If we haven't forgiven ourselves for something we have done, we may not forgive others so easily. And if we live in a state of gratitude for everyone and everything that is in our life, we will realize that all our relationships are just as they should be.

A woman moved to a new town and went to the general store to purchase a few items. While there, she told the gentleman behind the counter that she was new in town and asked him what the people in this area were like. He asked her what the people were like where she lived previously. The woman rolled her eyes and replied that she was happy to have moved because she found the people in her previous town to be small-minded, unfriendly, and bothersome. The gentleman frowned and told her that he was sorry to say that she would probably find the people in this town to be exactly the same. She left the store aggravated and upset.

The next day another woman walked into the store. She was also new in town and asked the gentleman the same question. When he asked her what the people were like where she lived previously, she got a tear in her eye. She said she was sad to have left so many wonderful, dear, kind, and thoughtful friends and neighbors and hoped that she would be able to make new friends quickly. The gentleman smiled at her and said he knew she would have no problem making friends because she would find the people in this town to be exactly the same. She left happy with this good news.

Wherever you go, there you are. We need to be aware of what we bring to the relationship table. How are we showing up? Are we a brokenhearted, sad, or angry victim? Or are we a joyful, light, and loving participant? Do we anticipate our friendships and relationships going right or going wrong? Are we in it for the long-term or for quick gratification? Do we project our fears or our fears onto others? There is no right or wrong answer, but it becomes obvious that how we show up can change the entire equation. The ingredients we toss into the batter can cause the entire cake to either rise or fall. And, rotten eggs make the batter taste quite nasty.

So what do we do with relationships that have challenged us? How do we look at them from a fresh perspective? And how do we attract more love into our lives? Try the five Ls of relationships:

LAUGH
↕
LET GO ↔ LOVE ↔ LEARN
↕
LIVE

These five Ls can help us get past the difficulties we experience, as well as attract more love. On the very top of the circle is laugh, otherwise known as having a sense of humor. This topic is so important to all of our relationships, and actually to all of life, that an entire future chapter is devoted to it. So hold that thought.

Going clockwise, we get to learn. It serves us best when we acknowledge that there is something to be learned or experienced from every relationship we encounter. The good and the bad become more subjective when we put the proper frame around them. Relationships can teach us so much about ourselves, about our likes, dislikes, strengths, and weaknesses. We can learn to be more loving and accepting and when to say yes or no. The lessons are endless. But we are responsible to participate in the experience in a way that benefits all.

So we must learn our lessons and move to the next step, which is live. Too many people put their lives on hold waiting for the perfect love to appear or for a difficult situation to clear up. They stop living while waiting for a resolution. Many go through the motions of their day, but the joy and excitement is absent. There is no passion. They think that when the "perfect partner" arrives or the "imperfect partner" leaves, they can finally live their lives. So much time is lost in the process of waiting instead of living. Here is a hint: we can live our lives fully and passionately even if our situations aren't what we consider ideal. That way, once they become "ideal," we will have even more to look forward to. Live fully and completely in the moment, and the rest will take care of itself. We will naturally attract incredible people and circumstances into our lives. We will attract love in abundance. And other delightful opportunities will appear as well.

Moving another step around the circle, we get to "let go." This is often a misunderstood concept but vital to healthy, loving relationships. Letting go doesn't necessarily mean that we have to let go of an entire relationship. It may mean letting go of a particular expectation (or all expectations.) It may mean letting go of the fantasy we had. It may mean letting go of our frustration, anger, fear, or annoyance. It may mean letting go of "should've" and "could've." And it may mean letting go of a direction and an idea that no longer serves us or our higher selves. Letting go involves trust that everything will turn out fine. When we finally dislodge our nails from the rock on the edge of the cliff, very often we realize we can fly. And for those of us who can't fly, we see that the drop wasn't as far as we thought and another path was waiting for us when we touched the ground.

One important form of letting go is forgiveness. To forgive means we have let go of the anger, fear, pain, and resentment that we have toward someone. It doesn't mean that we like or condone that person's actions. It just means that we will no longer harbor the feelings that are causing us pain. Without forgiveness, we can never truly love someone, including ourselves.

And this brings us to the center of the circle, which is love. Love is not just one step in the process. Love works throughout the entire process, and that is why the arrows go in both directions from love. That is also why it is in the middle. Love is not just the romantic notion of pink hearts and white roses. Love is the absolute absence of fear. It is the open, gentle, quiet experience we have when we stop coming from a place of needs and wants. It is what we feel when we have no expectations. It is the peacefulness of fully experiencing the here and now. And when we come from that place of unconditional love, we can see our relationships for what they really are. They are our connection to another person. Whether it is a romantic relationship or a family relationship or any other kind, we are connected to that person. And we can determine, from an unbiased, loving space, how that relationship fits into our lives. It is imperative that we make peace with all of our relationships, because no relationship ever ends. Some of them just change titles and even addresses. So make peace with them, for everyone's sake.

The five Ls of relationships are essential. We need to break habits that hold us back from our authentic lives. When we distracted ourselves with the minutiae of perpetual annoyances, we ended up missing the big picture. By staring at the small spot on the table linen, we miss the entire feast. And guess who is at the feast? Sitting around the table are all the extraordinary people we dreamed of meeting. They are there hoping you will take your eyes off of that tiny stain and join them in laughter, learning, living, letting go, and love. So practice the five Ls and enjoy the company of true, loving friends.

*_*_*_*_*_*_*_*_*

The things we look to find "somewhere else"
aren't "somewhere else" at all.
They are here.
They were always here.
We just didn't always see them.

The qualities we try to find in "someone else"
aren't in "someone else" either.
They are in us.
They were always in us.
We just didn't always recognize them.

The events we try to find "sometime soon"
aren't "sometime soon" at all.
They are now.
They were always now.
We just didn't always live them.

*_*_*_*_*_*_*_*_*

We'll walk together for a while, my friend
Maybe an hour…
Maybe a day…
Maybe a lifetime…
We'll laugh and tell stories
Pick apples and drink from fresh springs
We'll run through fields of flowers
And watch the stars at night
We'll sing songs and dream dreams

And tell the world how good it is to be alive
We'll walk together for a while, my friend
Okay?

*_*_*_*_*_*_*_*

While walking around town, I found a cute little vegetarian restaurant down a quiet side street in Northampton, Massachusetts. Looking at the menu on the door, I spotted several tempting dishes. It wasn't quite dinnertime yet, but with a click of a lock I was let inside and the first one to be seated for an early dinner. I picked a table by the wall, chose a salad and a "special of the evening" and started writing in my journal while I waited for the food to be prepared.

I must have had my head buried thoroughly in my journal, because I didn't notice two young women sit down a few tables away from me. I became aware of them when they started laughing loudly. And from that point forward, it was impossible not to take notice. It wasn't that they were loud or obnoxious. It was that they were enjoying each other's company so completely that it was a pleasure to witness.

It turned out one young woman was vegetarian while the other loved meat. One was quite grounded and earthy while the other was airy and silly. They dressed differently, spoke differently, and had opposite political beliefs. I couldn't help but overhear their conversations, as the restaurant was still empty and they were sitting so close. With each comment they made, it became evident that these two were like night and day.

I loved the questions they asked each other and the candid answers they gave. They were reveling in their differences and seemed to be discovering new things about each other with every question.

After a while, they realized I could hear everything they were saying and included me in their conversation. That's when I asked them how they met. I assumed they were new friend from the way they interacted. The surprise was that they had known each other for most of their lives. They had been neighbors and schoolmates since elementary school and had only recently been separated by different college choices.

I told them that I found this unusual, and they asked why. I said they seemed so different from one another and acted as if they had only recently met. They giggled and answered, almost in unison, that other people had said the same thing to them before. They both said that they treasured their friendship and their differences and never stopped being inquisitive of one another and their opposite choices in so many areas of life. They said they learned a lot from each other by being friends.

How refreshing! Many of us choose friendships with people who share common interests. Perhaps that is easier, and it reinforces or validates the way we live our lives. My lesson that day was to respect and find wonder in the choices of another without any judgment… and even call that person my friend, not my enemy. These two young woman taught me a lot about relationships that day.

*_*_*_*_*_*_*_*_*

May your light shine so brightly
That those who have not yet come to find theirs
Will be able to see their way through the dark

*_*_*_*_*_*_*_*_*

CHAPTER NINE

Hilarious Wholarians

I feel like I am diagonally parked in a parallel universe.
—Author Unknown

I am thankful for laughter, except when milk comes out of my nose.
—Woody Allen

Laughter is the shortest distance between two people.
—Victor Borge

NINE

Announcement:
The Time to Lighten up is Now!

Please, for the love of the world and all your relationships, stop taking *everything* so seriously. If we learn to LOL (laugh out loud) or ROFL (roll on the floor laughing) more often, we will feel healthier and happier. It's a proven fact. Making sure we get our minimum daily requirement of laughter every day is as important as getting any other form of nourishment.

So, are you happy at this moment? If you are—awesome! Please hold that thought while we get everyone else on the same page with us. Okay, for those of you who aren't happy right now, think of a time when you felt really happy and go over the details in your mind. Let yourself feel as if it was happening right now. Go ahead, smile, feel good, breathe, and be happy. Are you there yet? Can you feel it? Good. If not, rent a funny movie, listen to children giggling, make funny faces at yourself in the mirror, jump on a trampoline, spend time with a friend who has a good sense of humor, or watch some old *Monty Python's Flying Circus* episodes. A healthy dose of Michael Palin and his cohorts, or perhaps some Three Stooges, is certain to cure the blues!

Now, let's hope that everyone reading this is happy. That would be such a wonderful thing. Happiness has been proven to help you live longer and healthier. It helps you get along with others better. It makes life much more pleasant. And it attracts other happy people into your life.

Many people keep themselves from feeling happy and light-hearted because they are filled with worry. According to the *Merriam Webster Dictionary*, worry is an uneasy state of mind usually over the possibility of an anticipated misfortune or trouble. According to this definition, when we have a worry about something in our lives, we are projecting into the future and assuming an outcome that we do not want, like, or enjoy. There is unease and perhaps even fear that there will be unfavorable results in a given situation. We agonize over a possible ending. And, worrying can cause us to feel strangled or constricted. Plain and simple, worrying is not life affirming and generally does not allow for infinite possibilities. It can be consuming and draining.

Now, imagine if we could actually predict the future. Many of us would be extraordinarily wealthy, because we would know the winning lottery numbers before any drawing. We would have the names of stocks that increase in value rapidly. Besides that, we would never plan an important event on a rainy day or get stuck in traffic. Just imagine how different our lives would be if we had the ability to accurately predict the future. But this is fantasy, right?

So why do so many people feel compelled to predict the future in a negative or self-defeating way by worrying? It is socially acceptable to say, "I just know that the test results won't be good," or "I bet the bill for my car repair is going to be high." But, if we announce that we will live a very long and healthy life or that we expect a tremendous amount of money to come to us soon, people look at us like we are a bit daft. For some reason, it is perfectly acceptable to worry and be negative in our predictions but not to predict glorious things for ourselves and those we love.

Worrying is a habit. It is a behavior that is taught, and for many people, it is repeated frequently. Quite often it is rationalized by the idea that it is a "realistic" way of looking at a situation. But this is not true. Worrying closes the mind to so many potentially positive outcomes. It limits us to a belief that something bad will happen. And it constricts our possibility thinking.

Thankfully, there is an answer. Change the way we think. Transform our habit. When we worry, we agonize. And the opposite of agonize is *ezinoga*. Look at it in the mirror. E-Z-I-N-O-G-A. We can learn to practice ezinoga every time we start to worry, and we can make this our new habit. Reverse our worry. We can plan for positive and extraordinary outcomes. If things look bleak, say *ezinoga*! When we feel blue, sing *ezinoga*! When we are sure that life will throw us a nasty curve, shout *ezinoga*! Let *ezinoga* chase those worries away. Don't agonize, just *ezinoga*!

Keeping a good sense of humor is therapeutic and makes us feel good. When we remember to stay light in the midst of a storm, we can fly above the clouds. Laughter has been documented to help in the healing process by increasing blood flow. And we can attend laughter yoga classes now as well. So when we are down or troubled and we need a helping hand, remember to give a little giggle, heehee, haha, or a big old muahahaha to help the situation along. Sometimes our troubles melt away in the face of a loud belly laugh. And it definitely makes the good times even better!

*_*_*_*_*_*_*_*
Levity University
~Apply Immediately~
To Earn This Degree:
A PhD
In Hee Hee Hee!
*_*_*_*_*_*_*_*

Three flies, a moth, and a centipede
Came knocking on my door.
And when I wouldn't open up
They crawled along the floor.

They found a hole and came right in
They walked right past my feet
Until they came up to my couch
Upon which they took a seat.

The centipede said in a tiny voice,
"We've come to be a pest
Don't try to stop or hinder us
For pesting we do best."

And with that said the flies took off
To buzz around my head.
I yelled and told them all to stop
Until my face was red.

But they just laughed and buzzed some more
And then the moth joined in.
He flew around so many times
My head began to spin.

I saw the centipede don boots
And jump right off the couch.
He stamped upon my little feet
Until I screamed, "Ouch... OUCH!"

I limped on over to a chair
And sat myself right down.
Three flies, a moth, and a centipede
All saw I had a frown.

They realized that their fun was done
And I would stand no more.
They quickly got in single file
And headed toward the door.

Right through the holes they crawled again
Into the dark, dark night.
I breathed a sigh of great relief
As they disappeared from sight.

Then from outside I thought I heard
A tiny little song:
"Tra, la, tra, la, we like to bug
Nice people all night long."

Three flies, a moth, and a centipede
Would bother me no more.
I closed the hole with masking tape
And triple-locked the door!

*_*_*_*_*_*_*_*

Many years ago, a friend invited me to spend the weekend in her country house. I immediately agreed as I needed a break, and it would be nice to spend some time with her and her son. She had the best sense of humor and always made me laugh. The next Saturday afternoon, we drove north a few hours, and the stress of work and school dissolved with every mile and every smile.

Just before we got to her house, we stopped to get something to eat. We were served a delicious home cooked meal that tasted like Grandma had lovingly prepared it, complete with hot apple pie for dessert. My belly was full, and by the time we got to the house, we were all a little sleepy. But I didn't want to go to sleep right away because I wanted to see the house and the property. Besides, it was still light out.

Well, the place was magical. The interior had lots of exposed wood, and outside was a wee meadow right beside a little lake. As you lounged on the balcony, you felt like you were in your own little world. You couldn't see the neighbors on either side. While I was getting my tour, it began to rain. At first it was a nice gentle rain, but it got progressively harder and louder, and the already darkening sky got pitch black. There were no lights for miles, and no stars or moon could shine through that storm.

We decided to call it an evening, and I assured everyone that I would gladly sleep on the couch in the living room. It was closest to the wood-burning stove, which thankfully was generating lots of heat. My friend and her son went off to their rooms, and I covered myself with a blanket, listening to the rain and the wind outside.

With a full belly, a warm room, and a comfy couch, I fell asleep immediately. But after just a few minutes I heard a funny noise at the front door, which was only about fifteen feet from where I was sleeping. At first, I thought it was the way the wind was making the door rattle, but the noise became more persistent. The room was completely dark except for the faint glow coming from the stove. I could just make out the doorway as I listened to the scratchy, banging noise get louder and louder.

Suddenly, the front door popped open. I could feel the cold, wet wind blow against my face, and I saw a shadow in the doorway. No sound would come out of my mouth as I watched the shadow, low to the ground, come into the room. It moved slowly and quietly, but without any light I couldn't see what it was. All I knew for sure was that it was heading in my direction. Slowly, it was getting closer and closer. I didn't want to close my eyes because I wanted to see what was coming at me. And still I could not scream or shout. I shook under the covers, not knowing what was approaching me. As it got within two feet of the couch, I could just make it out.

At the exact same moment that I could finally see what it was, the shadow realized I was there. With one big leap it jumped on me and began licking my face with great abandon. It was so happy to see a human being. The shadow turned out to be a very cold and wet dog that had gotten lost in the rainstorm and was looking for shelter. The dog licked and wiggled, and licked and wiggled some more.

At first I became upset as questions went through my head. Who had let their dog out in this weather? Why wasn't the door shut properly? What if it had been a bear? What if I had been hurt? But the more I pondered the situation, the funnier it became. And the dog kisses really got me giggling. And the more I giggled, the more he wiggled! This poor little pooch was just so happy to be out of the storm, I couldn't be mad. And I actually started laughing out loud when I saw the humor in it all.

By this point, all the noise woke my friend and her son. They both came running into the room and turned on the lights to see what all the commotion was about. They recognized the neighbor's dog instantly but couldn't figure out how it had gotten into the house. I tried to tell them the story between fits of laughter and dog licks. It didn't seem as scary now that the shadow turned out to be an overly friendly pup. But as I told it, they were really amazed that I hadn't yelled for help.

Well, it seems that my new dog friend was thrilled with the way events had turned out. All he wanted on that cold stormy evening was to find shelter, and as it turned out, a warm couch to share with an animal lover. And that's what he got. He snuggled himself up in the blankets (after we toweled him dry) and settled in for the evening. It was a tight squeeze, but we fell asleep together, knowing we were both safe and sound.

*_*_*_*_*_*_*

Always look on the bright side of life… whistling…

*_*_*_*_*_*_*

.

SECTION FOUR

WHY IT MATTERS

Out beyond ideas of wrongdoing and rightdoing,
there is a field. I will meet you there.
—Jalaluddin Rumi

CHAPTER TEN

Imagine All the People...

You see things, and you say, "Why?"
But I dream things that never were; and I say, "Why not?"
—George Bernard Shaw

Alice laughed: "There's no use trying."
She said, "One can't believe impossible things."
"I daresay you haven't had much practice," said the Queen. "When I
was younger, I always did it for half an hour a day. Why, sometimes
I've believed as many as six impossible things before breakfast."
—Lewis Carroll

A fool-proof method for sculpting an elephant:
first, get a huge block of marble;
and then you chip away everything that doesn't look
like the elephant.
—Author Unknown

TEN

How good is your imagination? Can you imagine peace on the planet? Can you imagine peace in your home or at your job? Can you imagine peace in yourself? How about imagining larger balances in your bank account? Or a healthy and vital body? Can you imagine your energy levels high, your attitude consistently good? Can you imagine enough hours in the day to do all you want and still have time to relax and be quiet for a bit?

Albert Einstein said that imagination is more important than knowledge because knowledge is limited, while imagination embraces the entire world. With imagination, anything is possible! As children, we allowed ourselves to imagine without limits. We imagined ourselves as kings and queens, astronauts and doctors. We imagined that our stuffed toys could speak and that empty teacups were full of delicious tea. We imagined that a blanket thrown over some chairs in the middle of the living room was a tent in a magical forest. The family dog was a horse walking across the desert, and the picnic table became a raft in the middle of the ocean. Squirrels were spies and monsters lived under our beds. The possibilities were endless. And the energy was contagious.

When a group of children were playing, they all imagined these things together. It became real to all of them, and time flew by as they pretended to be other people in other places. No one wanted to go home to eat or sleep. No one wanted to miss a good time or a laugh.

As adults, we need to exercise our imaginations more. We need to get those imagination muscles back in shape and start pretending that the world is a magical, wonderful place to live. Only with that kind of vision will we be able to make the changes we need to make. Only with the understanding of our interconnectedness will we care enough to do anything about our challenges. And with our imagination, we will be able to see the ripples that move from us out into the world.

This is important because our thoughts, actions, and imaginations affect other people. There is no denying that, although many have tried. For years, smokers thought their choice to smoke didn't hurt anyone except themselves. Now we know how deadly secondhand smoke can be. People drink and drive and kill thousands of people every year because they didn't consider how their actions and intentions would change lives forever. But the good news is that the same principle also works in a positive way. Instead of a drive-by shooting, we can have drive-by blessings. Instead of holding up a bank, we can hold up our hands in praise. Instead of drowning our sorrows in a bottle, we can swim in the sea of love and kindness. All of these alternatives will have far better outcomes for us as individuals and for the rest of the world.

As we toss "junk" into the pool of our lives, let's remember to mind our ripples. Those ripples move from us through our thoughts, words, and actions. Yes, even our thoughts. Just because we can't see it or hear it doesn't mean it can't have an impact. Have no doubt, there is power in your intentions. Experiments have shown the power of prayer working on people who don't even know that anyone is praying for them. Those people on the prayer list had better medical outcomes than people who weren't getting special prayers. Then there are the experiments of Dr. Masaru Emoto, who has shown that specific words can change the structure of a drop of water so that when it becomes frozen it take on different shapes.

One of my favorite stories about the power of thought happened to me in the late '90s. I was experiencing a challenging time in my life and found myself short of funds. I sat at the table with my checkbook and a calculator and determined that I would be about $100 short that month. That's not a great feeling. I tried recalculating and again got the same result. It was late at night, and I was tired and didn't want to think about my finances anymore. So I turned out the light, got in bed, and thought, *Boy, I hope I get $100 soon.*

The next morning, on my way out the door to go to work, I checked the mailbox. I'm not exactly sure why I did that since the mailman would not have delivered mail overnight. But lo and behold, there was an envelope with my name on it. Inside was a handwritten letter from someone I knew. The note said:

> *Dear Katrina,*
>
> *As you know, my birthday just passed. I was fortunate to get many nice gifts as well as some money from my family. At first I thought of different things I could do with the cash, but then I realized that I would get much more joy if I gave it away. Please don't say no and accept this $100 as a gift that I really want to share with you.*

You could have knocked me over with a feather. Not even twelve hours had passed from the time I had thought about getting $100 and finding a crisp bill in an envelope with this letter. From that moment on, I never doubted the power of my thoughts and watched them much more carefully.

Using our thoughts and our imaginations, our compassion and our intentions, we create a world that is more extraordinary than we know. If we use these together with Wholarian Vision, imagine how we will change the world. Together we can imagine abundance for all, greater health and peace, more friendships, infinite love, joy, and balance, and boundless miracles. We can hold the space for a healthy planet, a compassionate society, enlightened individuals, and love, love, love.

*_*_*_*_*_*_*

In our imagination
We are boundless
We soar to the moon
Fly to the stars
Without limits
Without boundaries
Filled with love
For each other
And for the word
A deep and passionate love
Eternal

*_*_*_*_*_*_*_*

She was standing at the end of her driveway, four years old and determined. Her grandma was close behind to make sure that enthusiasm didn't cause those little feet to run into the street. Skylar noticed me immediately and called me over with great urgency.

"Please help me call the ice cream man," she pleaded.

I walked across the lawn and looked at her.

She was beautiful, with her wild curly hair, and big brown eyes that stared at me. She wore a yellow and orange sundress and was heavily adorned in the costume jewelry she had been playing with just before coming out to call the ice cream man.

The bracelets jingled and jangled, and since they were too big for her small wrists, she kept her arms at a strange angle. The necklaces she wore almost reached to her knees.

This was the most perfect ice-cream-man-calling outfit I could imagine.

Her grandmother explained to me that since it was an overcast day, they had been playing dress-up inside the house. From what I could see, this game probably consisted of taking Grandma's jewelry box out and putting on as many bracelets and necklaces as possible. I was surprised that Skylar wasn't wearing a pair of oversized high heels. I know that this is one of her most favorite things to do, especially if she is playing dress-up.

But, as it turns out, Skylar didn't finish playing before she suddenly and loudly announced that she wanted ice cream from the ice cream man. When Grandma tried to explain that they would have to wait until the truck was in the neighborhood, Skylar announced that she would call him.

No amount of explaining could dissuade her from walking outside and standing at the end of the driveway to call the ice cream man. They had been standing there for a few minutes when I joined them. Skylar again asked me to help.

So, together we sang out, "Oh, ice cream man, please come here. Skylar wants some ice cream."

We did this several times, sometimes loudly and sometimes softly. But after numerous attempts, there was no ice cream man in sight.

The gray clouds threatened to bring an afternoon shower, and we mentioned to Skylar that we could wait for the ice cream man on the porch or in the house. But she shook her head the way only a child can do without getting a headache. She stood her ground.

"No, I'm calling the ice cream man, and he is coming."

At precisely that moment, the familiar white truck turned the corner, playing its Pied Piper-esque tune.

Grandma and I both stood with our mouths slightly agape as Skylar calmly flagged the truck down. She knew exactly what ice cream she wanted (conveniently, it was in colors that matched her sundress). She ordered matter-of-factly, and upon being handed her treasure, she calmly said to the man in the truck, "Thank you for coming when I called."

Two seconds later, she turned around, walked to me, and took my hand. With those big beautiful eyes looking up at me she said, "And thank you for helping me call him."

We walked to the porch together and sat down on the steps. As I watched Skylar devour her ice cream, I marveled at her belief, her utter and complete belief, that she could call the ice cream man. There was no doubt in her mind that she could accomplish it, and she did.

This was her world, and she was creating her reality. And there was no ego involved. She didn't turn to gloat over her accomplishment. She didn't say, "Look what I can do."

Instead, she expressed her gratitude and went on with life as ice cream dripped blissfully down her arms and left pastel-colored puddles on the ground.

I have thought about that Sunday afternoon often, and I thank Skylar for the lessons she taught me. As adults, we sometimes need a child to remind us of the obvious. Children are so much closer to the essential truth. They haven't accumulated the baggage we've attracted over the years. And they have not gotten attached to it.

Since that day, I choose to see the world through the eyes of a child more often. I believe in a world where the ice cream man comes when called as I create my own reality. What an exciting new/old place to be.

Come join Skylar and me at the end of the driveway. We would love to have your company.

And, by the way, what flavor ice cream do you want? I think I hear the ice cream man coming now.

CHAPTER ELEVEN

BELONGINGNESS—CIRCLES OF ONENESS

Learn to regard the souls around you as parts of some grand instrument. It is for each of us to know the keys and stops, that we may draw forth the harmonies that lie sleeping in the silent octaves.
—Anonymous

Individually, we are one drop. Together, we are an ocean.
—Ryunosuke Satoro

A universal soul is peacefully blended in every soul.
—Yogi Tea Bag

ELEVEN

Abraham Maslow, the American psychologist, is perhaps best known for his hierarchy of needs. He determined in his studies that humans have five basic needs. He lists physiological needs, safety needs, esteem needs, and self-actualization needs on his pyramid.

And right in the middle of the pyramid is the need for love and belongingness. According to Maslow, humans need to feel loved and part of a community of some type. This could mean a club, an organization, a religion, a team, or even a family. Connections play an important role, and without them, there can be health consequences. People without a sense of belonging are often lonely and depressed. People with strong human connections appear healthier and happier.

Isn't it a great feeling to have people around us who love us and care about us? Let's imagine ourselves in the middle of a circle. In the vision, let's surround ourselves with people we are fond of. Perhaps they are our family members, friends, coworkers, neighbors, club members, worship acquaintances, business partners, etc. They may be people we see every day or people we only see occasionally. But the common element is that they are in our lives, and we are connected. We feel a sense of belonging with these people, but not as a possession. Rather it is a sense of belonging on the heart level. They make us feel special, needed, important, and loved.

Is this also part of the allure of being a celebrity? Many people are enthralled with the status of celebrity because, on one level, it seems to afford the ability to have a lot of money, wear nice clothes, get a great table at the restaurant, and hang out with rich friends. But more than anything, celebrities seem more connected and perhaps more loved. They seem to belong to lots of groups. They know more people and have a larger circle of influence. Down deep, we want to feel that same connection with as many people as possible. We want to know that when we say something, many people will listen.

With this said, it is no wonder that networking sites have become very popular. We are looking for more ways to connect with one another. We like having a lot of friends and acquaintances. We long to see and feel our similarities. And, on a deep-down level, we want to know that we are never alone. Isn't it fun to think that when we all started in the pea soup of creation (please insert the creation story of your choice here), we were cells dividing right next to each other and that we recognized each other and said hi. Even if we speak different languages now and practice different religions, we can forget all that and say, "Hi, pea soup partner! How has your journey been so far?" Networking sites allow us to do this with people from all over the world.

Facebook is a great example of a modern form of belonging. Whenever we want to find out how one of our friends is doing, we just to go to their page and read their status. It's common to see the following:

"Tough day at work, but now home relaxing."

"Having a brew at the pub."

"Yay! My sister had a baby girl. Mom and baby are doing well."

"Watching a great baseball game."

"Ugh… think I caught a cold from my kids."

"Sitting in the house, watching the rain, drinking a cup of tea."

"Going to sleep now. Night-night, friends."

It is fun to let those-who-care know what is happening in our lives. And it is equally fun to see how our friends are doing. It is a way of feeling connected in this ultra-busy world. When we are all being pulled in many different directions, and our friends and family don't live close by, these tiny snapshots can comfort and inform us. It is our modern form of staying in touch with the people we love and care about. It is a current form of a social circle.

But how about when Facebook didn't exist? How about a time before computers, phones, cars, newspapers, or even indoor plumbing? Before these incredible tools of communication, transportation, and modern conveniences existed, there were other ways to get information. There were other ways of feeling like we were part of community. And that's where the watering hole comes in.

Fortunately, I live just a few miles from a deep underground freshwater spring with wonderfully cold water. I bring my bottles to the spring about once a week and fill them up—rain or shine. Depending on my schedule, I get there at different times of the day, and almost every time I go, morning, afternoon, or night, there are other people there also filling bottles. Sometimes there are even lines of people waiting. But what I find so interesting is that not only are people filling up their water vessels, they are also talking and exchanging information and connecting with other people at the spring. It's as if the spring brings out the light-heartedness and curiosity in the people who stopped by.

This is probably what happened centuries ago, and perhaps even now in more rural parts of the world. Everyone in a community or small town would need to go to the community well, freshwater spring, or river to get water for the day since there was no plumbing. During a trip for water, one would get information. They could find out who was sick, who had a successful crop, what happened at a town meeting last week, what the latest weather prediction was, and so on.

So, the chore of getting water was also a way of gathering and disseminating information. We were able to check on the status reports of our circle of friends and acquaintances. We were able to find out about our neighbors and friends by word of mouth. If we didn't show up for a few days, people would wonder what was wrong and check on us. We felt like we belonged to the community. The watering hole allowed us to feel connected even before cell phones and online social networking.

Perhaps the water itself actually lends inspiration to this activity of connecting. We all need water to live. And we all need connection to thrive. Both are necessary in our human existence. Both are needed in our circle of life and Oneness.

*_*_*_*_*_*_*_*

The Well

There is a well so deep and infinite

The thirst of nations are quenched
And fires are drenched
All in need of cleansing are cleansed
With your cup, ladle, bucket, spoon
Dip it into the coolness
Refreshing, rejuvenating and restoring
Don't be shy… plenty for all
And available to all
Taste it, drink it, bathe in it
It is the water of life
It is the water of eternal love
Enjoy it for you will never tire of it
Tell all, tell all, tell all
It is for us to share
The water of deep and infinite love

_*_*_*_*_*_*_*

The Wholarian Vision is all about bringing people together. It is about celebrating our similarities as well as our differences. It is about smiling, waving and saying hello to our neighbors on our Facebook page, a watering hole, a church or temple, a classroom, or a bookstore. It is about reaching out to someone who may need a little laughter and a kind word. It is about doing something nice for someone without expecting anything in return. It is about introducing yourself to someone and making a friend. It is about knowing you belong, and creating the circle of Oneness.

*_*_*_*_*_*_*_*

There was never an agenda, and there were no set meeting times. We never exchanged phone numbers or addresses. Yet day after day, month after month, and year after year, we got together and shared what was in our hearts and heads. We sat in a circle at the bookstore, comforted by the knowing that someone would always be there to talk. Sometimes the topics were light and funny. Sometimes they were more serious.

Occasionally, a feather was ruffled, but most times it was just a sharing of ideas, thoughts, feelings, and laughter.

There was a unique bond between us. The group had people of different ages, sexes, and ethnicities. Some of us were there more often and some were just occasional visitors. People who walked by this gathering often asked if we were a club or a book discussion group. They wanted to put a name to our little circle. It would have been easier for "outsiders" to understand if something in particular brought us all together so regularly and kept us chatting for hours. But, as far as we were concerned, there were no outsiders. The moment anyone looked in our direction or said hello, they were one of us.

The sheer beauty of the group (if it can even be called that) was the absence of boundaries, demands, limits, rules, and regulations. All were welcome. All could participate. All were allowed their opinions. And all were permitted to just be. As a matter of fact, that was the glue that kept us together: the absence of judgment and the freedom to just be.

What a beautiful gift it was belonging with this circle of friends.

*_*_*_*_*_*_*_*

I was at a networking event a few years ago. There were about twenty participants, and we sat in a large circle. We began the event by going around the room introducing ourselves and speaking a bit about our passions. After each introduction, everyone else was invited to ask questions or make observations. There were so many wonderful and talented people at this gathering that it took a while.

I was one of the last people to speak. After I had introduced myself and said that I was an author and motivational speaker, a woman asked me a few questions and then said something quite interesting. She said that she saw me as a hub. I asked her to clarify her statement as I wasn't sure what she meant. She explained that to her, a hub was a person who not only knows a lot of people in different areas of life, but is also able to connect those people, the way a hub connects the spokes of a wheel.

That was an interesting and astute analogy from someone I had just met. And as I thought about it for a moment, I mentioned to the group that we were all hubs in our own way. We all know different people and connect them or bring them together in different capacities. I might be more vocal and visible in my approach, but we all serve as hubs. Many people in the circle agreed and saw that they also did that in their lives. Some disagreed and didn't see how they made those connections. So, I gave the example that even if you have just recommended your hairstylist or auto mechanic to someone, you have been a hub.

As a hub, we have our own unique circle of relationships. And they "belong" with us, not as a possession, but as a part of our crowd. It is comforting and makes us feel accepted and connected. We feel like we are part of something greater, which helps us get closer to that feeling of Oneness.

CHAPTER TWELVE

ONE SMALL STEP FOR WHOLARIANS

Talk doesn't cook rice.
—Chinese Proverb

Don't find fault. Find a remedy.
—Henry Ford

'Twas her thinking of others made you think of her.
—Elizabeth Barrett Browning

TWELVE

So how exactly do you bring almost seven billion people together in Oneness? How do you reassemble a vase that has been shattered into a million pieces? How do you start any task that seems insurmountable?

It all starts with One—one big smile, one genuine hello, one kind word, one sown seed, one small action, one embrace, one gentle thought, one moment of grace. If every person on the planet did just One thing… that would be almost seven billion things. There is another example of the power of One.

It is important to realize how many people we touch, literally or figuratively, every day. How many people do we affect with our moods, our choices, our words, etc? Take a moment right now and make a list. Write the names of all the people who live in your home (pets can be included). Next, write the names of all your friends and family members who do not live in your home but you keep in touch with regularly. Then write down all the people who live in your immediate area, either in your building or on your block. These are people you probably pass on a regular basis. Add the names of all the people you work with or go to school with. How about listing the people you see on a regular basis at the store, the gym, the doctor's office, the deli, the post office, and at religious gatherings? Do you belong to any clubs or organizations? Write down the names of those people. By now you may have anywhere from ten to one hundred names on your list, and there are more people whose lives you touch every day without realizing it.

We affect the lives of the people who plant, harvest, ship, package, and sell our food. We affect the lives of the people who weave, dye, cut, sew, ship, hang, and sell a garment. We may not know their names, but we touch their lives. If we look at it from that perspective, the list that we just made now exponentially grows to hundreds if not thousands of people that you touch directly and indirectly every day. This is powerful and humbling at the same time.

But what do we do with this information? How does this help make the pieces come together? Well, the next part of the assignment is to realize how much we have in common with each and every person in the world. It is easiest to start with the people on our immediate list, because the similarities are most obvious. We are either related, live in the same neighborhood, attend the same school, work for the same company, and so on. But what about people who don't seem to have anything in common with us? It may be more difficult with those people, so here is a list of things you may have in common:

Eating
Drinking
Breathing
Heart beating
Eyes blinking
Sleeping
Laughing
Crying
Dancing
Walking
Listening to music
Making music
Taking photos
Having faith
Loving
Caring
Wearing clothes
Not wearing clothes
Having birthdays
Traveling
Earning money
Looking at the moon

Celebrating achievements
Making friends
Being grateful
Reading
Gardening
Dreaming
Exercising

Spend some time with this list, and recognize that even those people who seem to have the least in common with us do some of the same things we do. They probably do *many* of the same things we do. This list could really go on for about twenty pages with things we have in common with many, if not most, people on the planet.

We generally tend to look at our differences instead of our similarities, unless we are on a date. That's right! Just remember the excitement after we had a date with someone special. It felt amazing. Our hearts beat a bit louder, our bellies felt fluttery, and we smiled from ear to ear. And what got us that excited? Perhaps the person was very attractive or smart or funny. Perhaps we shared a delicious meal or watched a great show. But the moments that probably got us most excited on that date were realizing how much we had in common. We may have found out that… we both like dogs, both have an aunt named Matilda, both dislike mushrooms, both grow our own vegetables, are both *Star Wars* fans, drive the same make of car, love the color blue, are both divorced, come from the same religious upbringing, both sneeze really loudly, both like roller coasters and Ferris wheels…

Let's face it. Lots of people may have these things in common. But when we are looking for a love connection, there is nothing like discovering that we have a lot in common.

So our mission, should we choose to accept it, is to make mini-love connections every day. This doesn't mean getting romantically involved with everyone we meet who dislikes mushrooms and loves Ferris wheels. But it does mean having a sense of excitement meeting people and recognizing that we have something in common, rather than just noticing the differences.

Just think, if we spent more time dwelling on our similarities, there would probably be fewer lawsuits because people would feel inspired to work things out together. There would be less illness because people would realize their health is important to everyone around them. There would be less poverty because we would take care of each other. There would be less loneliness because we would look in on each other. There would be more hope because we would all be working towards a better future.

And what happens when we keep noticing the differences? We love them too! After all, they are also part of the One. Differences don't make us bad, just... different.

The Wholarian Vision is really so simple when we remember our interconnectedness, our unity, and our Oneness. It is the Un-Wholarian vision that gets complicated and divisive. Let's remember that we share the same planet, feel the warmth of the same sun, and gaze at the same moon. And when we remember that, our differences won't make such a difference.

*_*_*_*_*_*_*_*

It's in an expression
In a stranger's smile
It's in the clouds
In the falling leaves
In a bird's song
And a butterfly's wings
It's in a laugh
In a tear
In a knowing look
In an instant
It's in everyone and everything
Everywhere
The One

*_*_*_*_*_*_*_*

When you were a child and saw Blessing walk into a room, you just couldn't take your eyes off her. She shined the way the sun shines through a window. And her light streamed into all aspects of her life. She was a peacemaker who never got into fights. If there was an argument, she would help everyone find an amicable solution. She had tremendous compassion. When she discovered toads or grasshoppers in the road, she picked them up and put them back in the grass so they wouldn't get hit by a car. Stray or wounded animals often traveled home with Blessing. Her parents let her use a room in the back of the house for all the creatures she helped heal before releasing them back into the wild. And she loved to connect with people. Blessing listened intently when anyone spoke to her, looking each speaker in the eyes. It was as if she was looking deeply into each soul.

She spoke softly, sang beautifully, and her sweet laughter was absolutely contagious. She rarely had the newest clothing but made everything she wore look pretty and fresh. There were often flowers in her hair or a pretty, meadow-flower garland around her neck. Blessing had wisdom beyond her age. Adults frequently were heard to say she was an old soul.

But as the years went on, Blessing realized she was different from other children. Some kids at school made fun of her because she was different, and she felt hurt and saddened by this. They teased her as she walked by. They made jokes about her and even called her names. She often went home with tears in her eyes. She didn't tell her parents because she didn't want them to be upset. So she sat in her room with the animals and sang to them or read them stories until she felt better. The animals always cheered her up. They always made her feel needed and loved.

Unfortunately, the teasing went on, and Blessing decided she wanted to blend in more. She didn't want to be so different from everyone else or feel so uncomfortable. She didn't like being called names. So she earned enough money to buy fashionable clothes. She stopped reading the books she liked and started to read trendy magazines so she could see how other people dressed, spoke, and acted. She emulated those people and quickly learned to blend in. She spent less and less time with her animals and more time with the popular crowd. She stopped wearing flowers in her hair and started using hairspray instead. The rosy glow on her cheeks was no longer from running around outside barefoot; she now bought it from the drugstore with the money she earned babysitting.

Blessing became more popular and went through high school and college with this new lifestyle. She made choices that weren't always wise, but she didn't care because she was no longer an outsider. And if everyone else was doing something, that was good enough for her. However, deep inside, Blessing knew something was missing. There was a part of her that recognized that she wasn't being authentic, and it made her sad. The beautiful, free-spirited child she once was was now locked away inside and was not allowed to come out. But she remembered how bad it felt to be made fun of and didn't want to relive that. So she continued to blend in with the world and all of its expectations.

It's no surprise that she married at an early age. After all, isn't that how all the stories go? Girl meets boy, they get married, buy a house, and live happily ever after. Right? Unfortunately, the marriage didn't work, and Blessing was left on her own to wonder why she wasn't able to create the "perfect" life she saw in all the magazines and on television. So she went back to school and earned another degree and dreamed of the day that she would be able to live the fairytale.

More years went by, and another man entered her life. They dated, spent lots of time together, went on vacations together, and after a while he asked her to marry him. She accepted. Blessing was so happy, because she felt needed and loved by this man. This would finally be her fairytale. She found her knight, they would have a home with children, maybe even a puppy, and life would be perfect.

They were together a few years and had their share of disagreements. Everyone said this was normal. But Blessing had a nagging feeling that there was something else wrong. She felt like she couldn't let her light shine too much or her husband would feel diminished. She couldn't express her own hopes and dreams because he wanted her to follow his. He didn't want to spend time with her friends or do the things she wanted to do. He had his agenda, and she could either follow it or go on her own. Blessing started to realize that she still didn't feel safe to free the bright, shining child inside her and had to hide it away even deeper.

One October day, Blessing went to work and filled her day with appointments and phone calls. But she was excited, because she would be going to dinner that evening with her husband to celebrate her birthday. They had been arguing a lot lately, but he wanted to take her out and have some fun. She felt lighthearted and hopeful. Unfortunately, that dinner was not to be.

Right before her last appointment, Blessing stood up from her desk to stretch her legs and realized something was terribly wrong. She felt dizzy and nauseous and tried to get to another room to lie down for a few minutes. But she passed out. An employee and a customer helped her stand up and walk to a chair. They brought her some water and called her husband, who worked nearby. He came as soon as possible and took her home. She felt tremendous pain and knew that they needed to call her doctor. Thankfully, the doctor agreed to meet them at the hospital. By the time they arrived, Blessing was unconscious and in shock. The doctor saw how serious the situation was and immediately admitted her. He diagnosed her and said he had to operate. If he didn't, she only had a short time to live.

You see, Blessing did not realize she was about seven weeks pregnant. Unfortunately, it was an ectopic pregnancy that had ruptured, causing two major arteries to hemorrhage. By the time she arrived in the hospital, she had lost about half her blood into her abdomen and was rapidly bleeding to death. By God's grace and the skill of her physician, her life was spared that evening. But nothing would be the same ever again.

They say that tragedy can either bring a couple closer together or split them apart. In this case, it did the latter, and within a few months, Blessing's husband asked for a divorce. With profound sadness, she tried to move on with her life, but the pain of the divorce and the loss of her unborn child were unbearable. She never felt so lost, alone, and disillusioned by the stories she had been told of happily-ever-after. Why was this happening again? What was she doing wrong? Wasn't she doing everything she had read in the magazine articles and seen in the movies?

A few months after the divorce, a chance encounter with a stranger— someone she met through a mutual friend—opened her eyes. Although she didn't tell her story very often or with great detail, Blessing felt compelled to tell this young man what she had experienced with her second marriage, the pregnancy, the emergency surgery, and, ultimately, the divorce.

The young man listened and didn't interrupt. After he heard the whole story he said, "Your child, although it was never born, came to you for that short time to give you a message. You need to figure out what that message is. All I know is, it must be pretty important if you almost died to receive it."

Blessing gasped. The truth of that statement was so profound, and it came from someone who barely knew her. He was right. That unborn child represented the child she had kept buried inside herself for so long. It was the child she was not allowing herself to know out of fear. It was the free spirit she had harnessed for decades so that she would not look "different" from everyone else. That child was her light, and she could not keep it hidden any more or it would die inside her, where it didn't belong.

She only saw that young man one or two more times after their discussion that day. But his impact had been felt. She began the work of reconnecting with her authentic self. Blessing was determined to reacquaint herself with the person she really was, instead of the false persona she presented to the world. She had to relearn her relationships with everything in her life. It was a lot of work, but it was so worth it. And once she was truly able to let her light shine again, she knew that nothing would ever make her hide it away. That light let her see things completely different, with greater joy and understanding. Simple things now took on deeper meaning. Life was no longer about pleasing the world. Life was about being pleased with the world.

And a funny thing happened. No one laughed when she wore flowers in her hair now. No one called her funny names or sang taunting songs. No one gave her strange looks or tried to diminish her. Instead, people began to realize that they too could let their light shine. They too could fill a room with their presence and not be afraid. By allowing herself to reconnect, Blessing showed those around her that they could do the same. The child within her was shining again!

AFTERWORD

Do you feel it? Do you feel the paradigm shift? If you are reading this page, chances are good that you do. And chances are you are already part of the solution.

Right now, Wholarians around the world are bringing people closer together. We are listening more; encouraging tolerance; joining groups that have similar visions; reading and writing books that guide us; joining conversations that support peace and sustainability; modifying lifestyles to "be" the change; avoiding drama; choosing health and well-being daily; researching alternatives that do less harm to ourselves, our communities, and the planet; saying hello to strangers; volunteering to help the needy; and doing so much more. Like a giant jigsaw puzzle, we are patiently connecting the pieces that fit together to create the big picture. And from where I'm standing, the picture is beyond our imaginations!

It is no accident that we live in such a remarkable time. We have the ability to communicate with more people, more quickly than ever before. Our circles of influence have increased exponentially through the internet and cell phones. And personally, I am humbled by the number of e-mails and phone calls I have received from so many people around the globe who are already doing all the things mentioned in this book and more. I have met people who are making a difference, and it makes my heart overflow. It is good to know we no longer have to feel alone, isolated, or strange because of our beliefs. There are many who are already on the Wholarian train. People are finding extraordinary ways to bring the world together, instead of divide it apart. And to all those people, I say thank you.

It seems as if a large percentage of the media would have us believe that this is not the case, and that all this goodness does not exist. I am not media bashing, but it is hard to overlook the fact that the majority of stories in the news are about sadness, violence, destruction, war, pain, depression, and doom and gloom. And, while it is natural for our hearts to hurt when we witness children starving, animals tortured, land devastated, humans in pain, and natural and man-made disasters… please don't let these events overshadow the greater good that is taking place. We don't have to pretend that these terrible things aren't happening, but we don't have to be overwhelmed to the point of inaction because of them.

Bringing the world together only seems like a monumental task, because we stopped remembering that we are already together. But we never stopped being part of the One. Most people have forgotten, but even that is okay. We will remind them. We will remind them that they came from the One and will always be part of the One. It cannot be otherwise. Our actions, our choices, our lives, and our voices are the message of One heart, One world, and One love.

To all the light-workers, the visionaries, the storytellers, the healers, the bringers of peace, and the messengers of love and joy, I express my deep gratitude and appreciation. You are holding the space for the healing to happen and the pieces to come together. Individually and collectively, you are the paradigm shifters. You are the Wholarian Vision. You are the power of One.

Blessings to you all!

ABOUT THE AUTHOR:

Katrina Mayer is an ordained interfaith minister and earned her doctorate in metaphysics from American Institute of Holistic Theology. She has an MS in communications from Iona College and a BA in English and general literature from SUNY Binghamton. She is also the author of *The Mustard Seed Way*.

Katrina lives on the beautiful north shore of Long Island, New York. She balances her day between writing, motivational speaking, and working as a corporate executive. In her free time, she enjoys long walks, discovering new raw-food vegan recipes, and playing with Totoro, the wonder cat!

To connect with Katrina and many other Wholarians, please visit these websites:

http://wholarian.ning.com
www.facebook.com/wholarianvision
twitter.com/Wholarian1

BIBLIOGRAPHY

Introduction:
Williams, Jay, Raymond Abrashkin, and Paul Sagsoorian. *Danny Dunn and the Universal Glue.* New York: McGraw-Hill, 1977.

Chapter One:
The Holy Bible. Revised Standard Version Containing the Old and New Testaments. New York: T. Nelson, 1952.

Laozi, and Victor H. Mair. *Tao Te Ching: The Classic Book of Integrity and the Way.* New York: Bantam, 1990.

Easwaran, Eknath. *Bhagavad Gita.* Boston, MA: Shambhala Publications, 2004.

Mohinder, Singh. *Guru Granth Sahib: The Guru Eternal.* New Delhi, India: Himalayan, in Association with National Institute of Panjab Studies, 2008.

Abdel, Haleem MA. *The Quran.* New York: Oxford UP, 2005.

"Big Bang." *Wikipedia, the Free Encyclopedia.* Web. Sept. 9, 2010. en.wikipedia.org/wiki/Big_Bang

"Twenty Interesting and Useful Water Facts." *All About Water—Read, Learn, and Know about Water.* Sept. 2010. www.allaboutwater.org/water-facts.html

Chapter Two:
"The Particle Theory, States of Matter, Changes in States." *Vertical.gif.* Sept. 2010. clickandlearn.org/Gr9_Sci/Particle_Theory.htm

Chapter Three:
Curtis, Chara M., and Cynthia Aldrich. *All I See Is Part of Me*. Bellvue, WA: Illumination Arts Pub., 1994.
"How Moko the Dolphin Gave Humans a Masterclass in Saving Stranded Whales"—Times Online. Sept. 2010. www.timesonline.co.uk/tol/news/environment/article3540973.ece

Chapter Four:
"Religion and the Brain: In the New Field of 'Neurotheology,' Scientists Seek the Biological Basis of Spirituality. Is God All in Our Heads?" *Newsweek,* May 7, 2001.
"Meditation: Take a Stress-reduction Break Wherever You Are." *Mayo Clinic Medical Information and Tools for Healthy Living—MayoClinic.com*. Sept. 9, 2010. www.mayoclinic.com/health/meditation/HQ01070

Chapter Five:
Discovery Health's "Fantastic Facts about the Human Body." *Discovery Health "Health Guides."* Sept. 16, 2010. health.howstuffworks.com/human-body/parts/facts-about-the-human-body.htm

Chapter Seven:
K1391—NY Senate Open Legislation; "Commending Humanity's Team for Its Dedicated Efforts to Promote World Peace," May 21–26, 2010. open.nysenate.gov/legislation/api/1.0/html/bill/K1391
"Tutu Signs Appeal Seeking U.N. Oneness Day," UPI.com." Sept. 9, 2010. www.upi.com/Top_News/2009/02/10/Tutu-signs-appeal-seeking-UN-Oneness-Day/UPI-58711234284241
"International Day of Peace, 21 September 2010." *Welcome to the United Nations: It's Your World*. Sept. 9, 2010. www.un.org/en/events/peaceday/2010/eventsglobal.shtml

Chapter Ten:
Emoto, Masaru. *Messages from Water: The First Pictures of Frozen Water Crystals*. Netherlands: Hado Pub. 1999.